Praise for *This One Wild Life*

"Abdou's memoir is not just brave — in her writing, in dissecting her own vulnerability, and in her willingness to share it with the readers — it's a literary instruction manual on how to be afraid and how to overcome it. But what is this peculiar, electric outline of bravery that Abdou explores? It's risk and the ability to push forward. This applies to hiking but it's also — forgive the cliché — a metaphor for life. This is why this memoir is unlike any other; through the story of facing her fears, Abdou shows us that we are much stronger than we think." — JOWITA BYDLOWSKA, author of *Drunk Mom*

"In this brave and intimate 21st century memoir, Abdou negotiates the whipsawing tensions between motherhood, selfhood, marriage, and public life in an age when secrets have never been harder to keep, social media can be a truth-teller's harshest critic, and not even Nature can be counted on for sanctuary." — JOHN VAILLANT, author of *The Golden Spruce* and *The Jaguar's Children*

"*This One Wild Life* is an absolutely heartwarming love letter to the beautiful, if sometimes bumpy, paths that lead into the outdoors — and to the profound connections that arise within a family that walks, between a hiker and their trail, and within a person themselves." — HARLEY RUSTAD, journalist and author of *Big Lonely Doug*

"Reading this memoir about a mother and daughter forging connections with the wilderness — and each other — is like going forest bathing: it will leave you feeling refreshed and restored, with a big smile on your face. *This One Wild Life* is written with great honesty, insight, and love. Nature needs more friends (and mothers) like Angie Abdou!" — MARNI JACKSON, author of *The Mother Zone*

Praise for *Home Ice*

"The author brings a novelist's eye to the story, telling it in first-person present tense; with its sharp characterizations and dialogue in place of autobiographical exposition, the book is a first-rate memoir and a fine example of narrative nonfiction. It's also a must-read for parents with youngsters who play organized sports." — *Booklist* Starred Review

"This is a lively, honestly written account of parenting that will resonate with readers who are fully involved in their children's sports." — *Publishers Weekly*

"This immersive memoir brings together the personal and a good dollop of research in sports psychology. Abdou writes with uncommon frankness about the raw moments of hockey momdom and her personal life." — *Toronto Star*

"A cleverly crafted memoir . . . Abdou's memoir explores universal themes: the challenges of parenting, of relationships, of finding balance. Throughout, Abdou's penetrating wit provides a humorous foil to the seriousness of the hockey machine . . . Far beyond a hockey memoir, *Home Ice* is about the wrenching decisions parents make in their effort to give their children the best start in life. Most of all, *Home Ice* is about love." — V*oice Magazine*

A Mother-Daughter Wilderness Memoir

This One Wild Life

Angie Abdou

ECW

Purchase the print edition and receive the eBook free. For details, go to ecwpress.com/eBook.

Get the eBook free!*
*proof of purchase required

Copyright © Angie Abdou, 2021

Published by ECW Press
665 Gerrard Street East
Toronto, Ontario, Canada M4M 1Y2
416-694-3348 / info@ecwpress.com

Editor for the Press: Susan Renouf
Cover design: Brienne Lim
Cover photograph: © SnelsonStock/Shutterstock

To the best of her abilities, the author has related experiences, places, people, and organizations from his memories of them. In order to protect the privacy of others, she has, in some instances, changed the names of certain people and details of events and places.

Library and Archives Canada Cataloguing in Publication

Title: This one wild life : a mother-daughter wilderness memoir / Angie Abdou.

Names: Abdou, Angie, 1969- author.

Identifiers: Canadiana (print) 20200385224 | Canadiana (ebook) 20200385283

ISBN 978-1-77041-600-0 (softcover)
ISBN 978-1-77305-714-9 (ePub)
ISBN 978-1-77305-715-6 (PDF)
ISBN 978-1-77305-716-3 (Kindle)

Subjects: LCSH: Abdou, Angie, 1969- | LCSH: Mothers and daughters. | LCSH: Outdoor recreation—Psychological aspects. | LCSH: Nature—Psychological aspects. | LCSH: Bashfulness in children. | LCGFT: Autobiographies.

Classification: LCC PS8601.B36 Z46 2021 | DDC C818/.603—dc23

ISBN 978-1-77305-758-3 (Audio)

The publication of *This One Wild Life* has been generously supported by the Canada Council for the Arts and is funded in part by the Government of Canada. *Nous remercions le Conseil des arts du Canada de son soutien. Ce livre est financé en partie par le gouvernement du Canada.* We acknowledge the support of the Ontario Arts Council (OAC), an agency of the Government of Ontario, which last year funded 1,965 individual artists and 1,152 organizations in 197 communities across Ontario for a total of $51.9 million. We also acknowledge the contribution of the Government of Ontario through the Ontario Book Publishing Tax Credit, and through Ontario Creates for the marketing of this book.

PRINTED AND BOUND IN CANADA

PRINTING: MARQUIS 5 4 3 2 1

For readers.

When I ask myself what distinguishes memoir from other forms of narrative, I always come back to intimacy. I hope you will read this book as a long, intimate letter from a good friend.

Thank you for spending time with my book.

Contents

One

My Girl

My girl never needed me. That's what I've always said. *This one came out of the womb ready for her first year of college*, I'd joke. She arrived all fair skin and red hair, detached and regal, self-contained, like an entirely different species than her two-year-old brother, a case study in need.

As a baby, Ollie consumed me. "You're too responsive," people told me. "Let him cry it out." "You have to put him down." "You're spoiling him." I read the experts and studied my boy's cries, straining to decode the meaning of each whine and wail. Was it short or long? Sharp or dull? Urgent or passive? Did it mean hunger? fatigue? discomfort? illness? *Please. Just tell me: I'll fix it.*

But every cry seemed to mean one thing: *Pick me up, pick me up, pick me up.*

And never, ever put me down.

My girl made no such demands, and I accepted her self-sufficiency with gratitude and relief. Even their very births were fundamentally different. Ollie came to us via C-section, like a parcel in the mail. He wasn't there — for *weeks* after his due date, he still wasn't there — and suddenly he was there. His arrival seemed as simple as a nurse putting up a sheet, a masked man appearing on the other side, and *voila*: baby. My husband, Marty, didn't do well with the rapid transition. The doctor held up our new infant and announced in a booming voice: "IT'S . . . A . . ."

The doctor intended for Marty to examine the evidence on display and finish the sentence. Perhaps the doctor always did this: presented the father with the honor of revealing the tiny infant's sex to the new mother. Marty later told me that in the stress of the moment, in those very first seconds as a father, the only thing that came to his mind was . . . *Scrotum? It's a scrotum?*

The silence stretched until the doctor felt compelled to rescue Marty. "A BOY!" *It's a boy.*

Our daughter's birth allowed us time to brace ourselves for the before-and-after chasm that accompanies the arrival of a whole new human being. After a night of strenuous labor, my husband and I had transitioned to a world where we had two children. The new baby, a punctual and well-behaved creature from the beginning, burst onto the scene at exactly seven a.m. on her due date. When the doctor commanded me to push, I took up the challenge with intense focus, forgetting to breathe at all toward the end. A long-distance swimmer with decades of underwater-swimming practice, I could hold my breath for a very long time. The healthcare team whisked my oxygen-deprived newborn off to an incubator for a couple of days' recovery, but not before I got to see her.

She had nothing to do with the names we had picked out. All our zippy Zadie and Zoe options evaporated in the face of this calm queen-like creature. Marty and I fretted over names for two days before settling on the classic Katherine Elizabeth. Because Elizabeth came from my grandma, we threw in Marty's grandma's name too: Katherine Elizabeth Jean. A big name for a little baby.

"One thing I should tell you, Ang."

Uh-oh. "Yes?"

"You remember Katherine?"

Of course I remembered Katherine, Marty's ex-girlfriend, the one he was dating when he and I first met, first got drunk and had sex on someone's lawn at training camp in Fort Lauderdale, first fell in love. "Yes, I remember Katherine."

"Her middle name is Elizabeth. *Katherine. Elizabeth.*" He stressed each name as if in my post-partum bliss, I might miss the connection. His girlfriend. Our daughter.

Despite the possibility that Marty's ex would think we named our child after her, Katherine Elizabeth Jean stuck. I've never met a Katherine I didn't like.

Already in those earliest days of Katherine Elizabeth Jean's existence, I could feel the fluid and fast details of life hardening into narrative: my euphoric insistence that I loved giving birth and wanted six babies; the South African doctor assuring Marty that of course a forty-year-old woman, mother of a newborn and a toddler, didn't really want six more babies ("They all get a little crazy after the birth. Take her home. She'll settle down."); the stranger walking the hospital halls with a tiny, dark-haired creature tucked into his chest and his shoulder ("This is the best part of life," he told Marty. "Our fourth, and still: the very best part."). Before I'd even left the hospital, I'd already begun repeating stories, committing them to memory, weighting them with significance.

By the time the nurses brought me my redhead so I could finally hold her, I'd recovered from a night of missed sleep, and baby Katherine Elizabeth Jean had learned to be alone. We seized upon that self-reliance — a useful skill in a second child — as her defining characteristic. Ollie went to daycare during that first year of his sister's life, and our angelic girl slept beside me all day long while I wrote, completing a PhD dissertation with unexpected ease. The months galloped by, and soon she was looking up at me from her bassinet, declaring with perfect clarity: "Poor baby tired, milky night night."

"Um, did that baby just ask to go to bed?"

"Well, yeah," I would laugh. "Poor baby is tired. She wants her milky night night." I would give her a bottle, tuck her in, and not see her again until morning.

The first time I took her to a story-time circle, the leader read us a counting book. In a pause, my sweet little baby clapped her hands together and said "Onetwothreefourfivesix seveneightnineten." Any response I could think of felt like a brag, so I continued to stare straight ahead, waiting for the reading to continue, but I did hear the mother behind me whisper: "That's not right. That baby just counted to ten."

I can tell these kinds of stories about my daughter ad infinitum. The way she coordinated her outfits for school with such confidence (even if the coordinates made sense only to her own creative mind), the way she straight-lined down steep mountains by the age of seven while I skied behind her yelling *slow down*, the way she always refused offers of help with a firm "I do it."

We took her on her first overnight tenting trip before she turned two, and she did so well we named her Katie Camper Super Duper. After each subsequent success, we added to her name. Katie Camper Super Duper Awesome Skier. Katie Camper Super Duper Awesome Skier Tidy Printer. Katie Camper Super Duper Awesome Skier Tidy Printer Brilliant Artist. Within weeks, we struggled to say the name in one breath. By the age of three, it took us nearly a minute to pronounce the whole thing.

I wonder when I first realized the inadequate — one might even say fictional — nature of these stories that I tell about my daughter. When did it begin to enter my consciousness that our children are not really *ours*? From the earliest moments of her life, I created a version of "my girl" that had nothing — or at least not everything — to do with the complex, shifting, contradictory, autonomous, sometimes impenetrable, and ultimately unknowable human being we try to hold together with one simple word: Katie.

Two

Shy Katie versus Brave Katie, and Other Fictions of Selfhood

The shift happens for me — I don't pretend it has anything to do with her — partway through Katie's second grade. We've moved the kids to a new school, for Ollie's sake rather than Katie's, but we know we'll find it easier to have them in the same spot. Marty and I are not the type to make parenting look easy; we take the simplest route when we can. Besides, Katie has always proved to be less resistant to change than her brother: she'll love the new school, we tell ourselves.

Except she doesn't; not really. Things seem to go okay-ish during that tail-end of second grade, with everything brand new and teachers expecting her to be a little timid, but early in third grade we start getting notes from the school. Katie's shyness has become a problem.

"Katie's shy?" This comes as news to me. I don't believe it. *My* Katie? Katie Camper Super Duper?

"Of course she's shy," Marty says, with a hint of annoyance. *You should know this* is what I hear in his tone. "She's always been shy."

Marty and I have taken a divide-and-conquer approach to parenting. He had no interest in traveling for Ollie's hockey, so I tackled the unenviable role of hockey mom while he stayed home and took Katie skiing. The division got so deep that a reader of my recent memoir, *Home Ice: Reflections of a Reluctant Hockey Mom*, commented that Marty and I had already separated and taken up single parenting, despite living under the same roof. I looked at this reader, a man I'd never met before, a man who did not know my husband or either of my children besides what he'd learned in the pages of my own book, and I nodded. That's exactly what had happened to my family: divorced under one roof.

Now here, a season later, I face the results. I don't want to admit that Marty knows our daughter better than I do.

The concerns from school build. Katie doesn't like to go to the library alone, claiming she doesn't know how to find it and needs a classmate to accompany her.

"Well, if her sense of direction is as bad as mine, she might be telling the truth."

I always have an answer.

I look at the way she dresses — a startling clash of sparkling sequins and screaming colors — and assure myself: a timid kid does not design her outfits explicitly to draw attention. To me, everything about Katie exudes self-confidence.

But the school counselor and teachers continue to articulate their case. "Katie won't go to the school office." "She's afraid to talk to the secretary." "She rarely speaks in class." "She avoids all eye contact." "Her voice is so quiet nobody can hear her." "She has made few friends."

"It's true," Marty says. "In public, she's not the same kid we see at home. Out there, she ducks behind me, won't answer for herself. She's painfully shy."

"She needs more time with me." The thought comes to me fully formed, loud and clear. Of course she hides behind Marty at the ski hill. *I* would hide behind Marty at the ski hill. Any girl would duck behind this strong and confident man surrounded by skiing friends, completely in his element.

I deliberately organize the days to ensure I do more with Katie, and I start to see the pain of the "painfully shy" diagnosis. In public, she folds in on herself, willing herself smaller, trying to disappear. She speaks as if she hopes *not* to be heard. Where has my Katie Camper Super Duper gone?

"Don't worry about it," Marty says. "Lots of kids are shy. I was shy. You were probably shy. Of course kids are different at home than they are around strangers. It's fine."

Research tells me that Marty is right: many children do experience shyness. It can be caused by a variety of factors, including genetics, personality, learned behavior, lack of social interaction, harsh criticism, and fear of failure. However, through my turn to the experts, I also learn that such shyness is not always "fine." When the timidity begins to interfere with basic enjoyment of social situations, parents ought to seek help from a counselor or psychologist who can treat the condition with stress management, relaxation strategies, talk therapy, or social skills training.

Katie and I talk about her shyness. I begin with the laziest parenting strategy: bribery. I have an upcoming trip to France and know Katie wants to join me. She's started French immersion at school and, with an eye on my travel itinerary, she practices one phrase over and over again: "Je voudrais un croissant au chocolat, s'il vous plaît."

"Well, I'm sure you do, but would it be fun for someone so *shy* to travel to France?" My smile presents the statement as a friendly challenge. "Maybe we should wait until you're feeling more comfortable and outgoing and can *enjoy* the adventure of new places and new people."

Katie shouts her response, leaping off the ground with a smile to contradict my assessment of her. "Me?! Shy?! I'm not shy!" And there she is, all lit up, my happy and confident Katie.

Of course, her reactions to my bribes never stick. Back in public, the spark of loud self-assurance passes. Katie dims.

"Do you know the reason I want you to overcome this shyness? I want everyone else to see the Katie I see. It's not fair to them. The 'you' I see is filled with brightness and energy and life. But nobody else gets to see that Katie. You turn your light off for them. Think of driving in the car — we zip right past a dark house without even noticing. That makes me sad, to think of all the light that people will miss when they don't get to see you."

I declare the school break between third and fourth grades "The Summer of Mommy and Katie." We do everything together: hiking, biking, swimming, reading, rafting. We name ourselves Smoke and Fire: "Fire" in reference to Katie's auburn hair and "Smoke" to describe my own hair, recently turned to ash. We create a secret handshake: "Where there's Smoke, there's Fire. Where there's Fire, there's Smoke." Clasp, clasp, punch, flutter. We perform our handshake at the start and finish of every hike, holding hard eye contact. I begin to draw on the Smoke-and-Fire ritual any time I want to connect with my daughter, any time I need to say *I see you and I'm here for you. Always.*

Marty and Ollie roll their eyes at our ritual.

"You guys are so cool. Well, we have nicknames too," Marty says, crossing his eyes and shaking his hands in an awkward hang loose at Ollie. "Thunder and Storm."

"You can't make up your own nickname, Marty."

"Oh, okay then, whatever you say, *Smoke.*"

I want to say that I never chose the name Smoke for myself, but we'd both recognize the lie. Marty had not been a fan of my decision to go grey, and this nickname emerged as my attempt to embrace the change, to celebrate middle age, to find confidence in my au naturel look.

"And anyways," Ollie jumps in, happy to join Team Thunder and Storm, "you *can* have smoke without fire."

Marty shoots him a quick power punch. "You can also have fire without smoke."

I see in the kids' smiles that they take as much pleasure in this jovial ribbing as Marty and I do. The playful banter comes with no true animosity. Marty and I have recently slogged our way out of a particularly bad patch in our marriage. After a few years of staying together for the kids, and then staying together for the mortgage, we arrived at a point where we had only one sensible course of action: divorce. Our regular arguments — animosity verging on hatred — made our home an unhealthy and stressful place, especially for two young and sensitive kids. In the nauseating grip of guilt, I read a slew of articles written by psychiatrists who argued that chaotic homes and marital discord can lead to shy or anxious children.

Out there on the precipice of divorce, knowing that staying together (for anybody) no longer made sense and that the stress of our marriage would soon blow the whole house apart, Marty and I finally saw each other again. I remember my "oh, it's *you*" moment. *You*: the long-limbed, lithe butterflyer from my university swim team, the one who gave perfect post-race neck massages. *You*: the adventurous friend who introduced me to the serenity and joy of backcountry mountain adventure. *You*: my partner through the miracle of two childbirths, late enough in my life that I'd nearly given up on motherhood. *You*: my best friend of over two decades, who eventually grew to know and understand me better than anyone, perhaps even better than I know and understand myself.

You.

"Well, I love you," I thought, just in time. "I'm not going to lose you."

Teetering on the brink of divorce, we chose each other anew — for one reason alone: our deep and long-standing connection to each other. We found the version of "us" worth saving. Admittedly, the rediscovery came after many hard conversations and a whole lot of labor-intensive breaking of bad habits, but Marty-and-I emerged, still together and as happy as newlyweds. The resulting lightness in our home comes as such a relief — to all of us.

Katie and I do not let the boys' teasing dissuade us from our season. Fire and Smoke don't care about anyone else's opinion. We do our handshake and head out on our next adventure. Katie comes alive that summer, blooming in the sunlight of her mother's gaze. I love to watch her smiling and laughing, initiating conversations, holding her head high while telling a story in a loud, enthusiastic voice. But I also feel annoyance at myself, even the familiar skin crawl of shame. Why has it taken a scholastic crisis for me to acknowledge that a girl needs her mother's attention? Why had I been so ready to shuffle Katie off to her father while I worked to meet my son's needs? Once things went wrong at school, I easily intuited that Katie most needed some simple one-on-one time with me.

In *The Emotionally Absent Mother*, psychotherapist Jasmin Lee Cori argues that "Mother is the axis around which the family and the child's emotional life revolve." Emphasizing that no mother will be attuned to her child one hundred percent of the time, Cori cites studies that show much less time will do. Dr. Ed Tronick, a child development expert, claims even attentive parents can only be attuned to a child's needs approximately thirty percent of the time. However, those children spend much more time attuned to their parents, observing our behavior, absorbing our emotions. Cori emphasizes that a mother does not need to do the right thing all the time, as long as she puts in the effort to make things right when she misses.

Rather than feel distressed at the research about a mother's role in the happiness and well-being of her children, I feel empowered. Perhaps I have "missed" with Katie over the last couple of years, but it's not too late to make it right. An outgoing female role model, some kind motherly encouragement, a space in which she feels comfortable to let herself shine — that will turn this timidity around. Goodbye, meek Katie.

In the breaks from our mother-daughter outings, I tear through parenting magazines and scholarly articles, expecting profound insights on the nature of gender and rectitude, hoping for clear and helpful advice. I find alarming warnings that shyness can lead to anxiety and fear, which can then result in social isolation and depression. I read that shy children run the risk of bullying and rejection and have a hard time making friends. I learn that girls tend to learn most of their behavior from imitating their mothers. The expert *advice?* I unearth only two practical, helpful pieces of that: 1) don't try to force children out of timidity, but make a receptive, encouraging space for them to enter when ready; and 2) don't use the word *shy*, which a child will accept as a statement of personal defect.

Since that very first phone call from Katie's school, conversations at our house have been regularly punctuated by one word: *shy*.

I take note of the advice to be more selective about our vocabulary, but otherwise the research doesn't offer much insight or suggested practice. I'm an academic by training and profession, and I feel compelled to read the experts, but I don't often find transformative revelations there, nothing that I can't come up with during a good coffee date with a smart, empathetic friend. So I make a steaming cup of peppermint tea, wrap myself in a giant white afghan knit by my grandmother, chase everyone out of the room, and curl into my favorite chair to call Gyllie, possibly my smartest and most empathetic friend.

Gyllie and I met on our first day of graduate school. Most of my best friends come from those earliest adult years, and we occasionally wonder why we don't tend to make the same kinds of friends once we move out of our twenties and into proper adulthood. Partly, once we land in the busiest years of our lives, we don't have the luxury of time to find and make new friends. There is an easy comfort in feeling more *known* to these old friends: We don't have to explain ourselves. We no longer need to describe our parents, our childhoods, our early romantic relationships, or our professional failures. We can skip backstory. With new friends, each time we begin to share these stories, as a way of creating ourselves for them, we put a spin on the past, maybe take it a step further from what actually happened. Old friends, I believe, can catch glimpses of knowing somewhere out beyond story and language. We bring a sense of all those formative experiences — and the ways they've manifested in the many years we've known each other — to an understanding of each new experience, without having to retell (and inevitably reshape) the past.

For nearly three decades, Gyllie and I have known each other that way. We've lived on opposite sides of the continent for far longer than not, but the physical distance has never threatened our friendship. This past winter, when Gyllie joined me at a literary event in Northern Ontario, I introduced her to my co-speaker, Karl Subban, saying, "Gyllie and I have been together through three marriages, four degrees, five kids, three cross-country moves, six cats, four dogs, and seven jobs. Husbands come and go, but Gyllie is stuck with me."

I've turned to Gyllie in the bumpiest parts of my life: when I dropped out of my first PhD, when I left my first husband, when I suffered a life-altering injury in a nearly fatal car crash, and when I almost let go of my second marriage. After I had kids, I took comfort in knowing Gyllie had traveled that road first.

On the phone, she and I meander, swapping stories of our lives, the leisurely pace an old-fashioned luxury. We weave talk about books and kids and work and husbands. I've been reading Karl Ove Knausgaard, a Norwegian sensation who's published a nearly four-thousand-page series of autofiction.

"*My Struggle*, it's called. Fitting."

"Why read it if it's a struggle?"

"I heard so much about it, this guy writing about every banal detail of his life. The massive international success made me curious. Why does everyone care? Then after I read book one . . . I don't know . . . he's doing something new. I want to have an opinion about it. I hate people having opinions about books they haven't read." Gyllie laughs. She knows this hatred has almost everything to do with responses to my own books. "So I'll read the whole damn six-book series, and *then* I will have an opinion." I'm in the middle of the fifth book, and the undertaking has started to feel like a serious commitment. A relationship of sorts.

"But why read about some guy cleaning his teeth and changing his kids' diapers? Isn't it boring?"

"Sometimes boring. Sometimes shockingly honest. He gets my heart racing from sheer discomfort, wondering: *how can he write this for the whole world to see?* Or, *what must his family think?* Or, *how can he do this to his wife?* Or, *doesn't he care what people think of him? Does anyone he loves even talk to him anymore?*" The more honesty in his scenes, the more I realize that we're often not honest in real life. There's so much we don't dare say. *My Struggle* replicates real life, but without the filters and the social niceties. "Sure, though, yes, lots of boredom too. Like life. I heard Knausgaard say in an interview that he writes fast to escape narrative. Like if he doesn't shape his life and polish the events into smooth story, he can capture something more true, escape the falsehoods inherent in storytelling."

"Uh-huh. And does he?" Gyllie puts the answer in her question. Of course he doesn't: escaping narrative is impossible. In attempting to understand our own lives, we shape incidents into story — we decide what to include, what to exclude, what inter-pretive spin will work best. In the name of making meaning, we depend upon the lie of narrative.

I suspect Gyllie enjoys getting my short take on the Knausgaard series because she's too practical to waste months on a male narcissist.

"But he's smart," I tell her. "That makes a difference."

I wonder how much to tell Gyllie about the book I recently finished, the fourth in the series. It focuses on Knausgaard in his late teens. He completes school and travels north to work as a teacher in a remote village, planning to save money and become a writer. His primary goal, though? Losing his virginity. He drinks a lot to gain the confidence to approach girls. His main obstacle presents itself not in the form of reluctant partners, but in his own tendency to premature ejaculation. In the final chapter, he finds a young woman willing to have sex with him not just once but several times in a quick succession, the repetition helping him pro-long his own release. I relay this plot to Gyllie as briefly as I can and tell her, "The book ends with the young woman so drunk that she leans out the tent to throw up, and Knausgaard, unable to resist her bare rump in the air, begins 'pumping away yet again.' That's the final image."

"Pumping away?!" Gyllie chokes on her coffee. Laughter is my favorite part of visits with Gyllie.

"His words. He does not try to make himself appealing, trust me. But he still shapes. Even the choice where to end, that's nar-rative, right?" The simple — and necessary — decisions of where to start and where to end prove Knausgaard, like all writers, like everyone, a prisoner of narrative.

"It sounds like literature for the selfie age. Me, me, me."

"Sort of," I answer. "But maybe a parody of the selfie age. Selfies are all about good filters and flattering angles. Knausgaard uses blunt angles and the harshest light." I think about selection too. On social media, we curate our lives for others. The sheer length of Knausgaard's series makes it seem entirely uncurated. Perhaps the series reflects our age's obsession with the self taken to its farthest-flung conclusion, but it also reflects Knausgaard's ideas about writing taken to their extremes. The honesty about what it feels like to be alive right now breathes life into any narrative. By that criteria, why not skip the pretense of fiction altogether? That's what Knausgaard does: puts himself on the page, naked.

After we exhaust our book talk, Gyllie tells me about her kids. I pull my dog, Blue, onto my chest as Gyllie talks, rub my face in his fur.

Katie's friend Jaimie once told me, in her sweet, pointed way, "*We* wash our dog every week. So he *doesn't* smell." She wrinkled her nose in Blue's direction.

"That's what I love about Blue," I told her. "He smells like dog."

Now I put my nose deep in his thick mane and breathe him in. A bundle of nature, a piece of wild.

"Katie and I have had a great summer," I tell Gyllie. "I'm thinking of taking her up Mount Fernie next weekend. Before she's back to school." I pick Blue's shedding black hair off my Grandma blanket (as I call it when I'm at my darkest and need its comfort: *someone please bring me my Grandma blanket*). Gyllie expresses no surprise at Katie's hiking feat. I could announce that nine-year-old Katie plans to tackle Everest, and Gyllie would ask when we're leaving. "We've been doing lots of activities, mother-daughter outings, to build her confidence," I add, testing out this new version of my daughter on one of my oldest friends. "Katie had some problems at school last year. She's really shy." Even as I say it, I'm not sure I believe in this shy Katie, not fully.

"*Katie is shy?*" I understand the disbelief in Gyllie's voice. Gyllie knows Katie only from my emails and texts, the invincible and flashy Katie of Facebook, the Katie I have constructed out of bits and pieces of our life: an energetic photograph, an inspiring story, a precocious quotation, a lively performance on video, our own carefully curated social media image.

I'd like to think I didn't make that Katie up from nothing, that the Katie I represent on Facebook is one I see because she exists too.

The school counselor, a dynamic and brilliant woman widely adored, uses similar language: the same dependence on dualities, the same notion of competing Katies. She tells my daughter to imagine a Shy Katie and a Brave Katie, and to refocus her attention and belief on the latter. "Draw a picture of Brave Katie," she says. "Tape her to your mirror."

As the Summer of Mommy and Katie turns to talk of fall outfits and school supplies, I begin to believe in the counselor's strategy. Katie clears a space in her messy room — and in her imagination — for Brave Katie. She summons Brave Katie more often, offering to do simple public tasks by herself. She walks down to the grocery store to buy bread without us. Afterward, the tellers laugh about Katie's quiet voice — "We could barely hear her!" — but still Brave Katie does it.

Katie and I tackle Mount Fernie in the final week of August, right before she starts fourth grade. I like stories more than numbers, and I am most aware of my own ineptitude when people ask me the elevation of my town or its ski hill (how should I know?), but a guidebook tells me Mount Fernie qualifies as a half-day advanced hike, four kilometers each way with a nine-hundred-and-forty-five-meter elevation gain, two thousand and twelve meters at its summit. A local mountaineer describes it as "a good, stiff hike."

I don't set out committed to doing the whole thing, and as we get going, the top seems less likely. The beginning of the trail is steeper than I remember. Within ten minutes, we're both huffing. Little Blue runs up and back, through the bush, around our feet, dashing ahead on the trail until we can't see him anymore and then bolting out of trees behind us, round and round, a wide smile on his tiny fox face. His solid black coat and thick mane mixed with miniature size and sharp facial features make him look like a cross between a fox and a wolf; a wox, we call him. I worry he'll startle other hikers who will be on high alert for wildlife, but I can't bring myself to rein him in.

"How does he have so much energy?" Katie pants, taking exaggerated slow steps up the mountain, toe-dragging one foot behind her and then the other, coming to a dead halt to pick thimbleberries, sucking her cheeks in at their tang.

"This hike is funny, I remember now. It's difficult right at the beginning, when you're not warmed up, before you're expecting it." I trail my fingers through the back of her damp curly red hair. "I'm sweating too, but we'll hit shade soon, and I think the trail levels out a bit. Let's try to make it to the bench?" I remember a plank between two trees about halfway up. It has an expansive view that makes me believe in God: nothing but wilderness in every direction, three ragged rocky peaks glistening in the sun, a thick emerald carpet of infinite forest. These first fifteen minutes have been so effortful that the bench seems an ambitious goal for today.

But Katie's response surprises me. "I want to make it to the top." She has a pinched determination in the triangle between her eyes and nose, a quiet seriousness in the tight line of her mouth. Her intense focus reminds me of Marty. She's resolute. *Resolute.* I like the way the word rolls in my mouth. It's an adjective I've never used of myself.

"The top? Yeesh," I say, uncertain. "It's high. And far." I point to the black clouds on the horizon and do a quick inventory of my CamelBak: minimal snacks, no rain jackets, no sweaters. Marty usually brings us on our adventures; I've come to rely on his obsessive preparedness. I'm relieved to remember that I did, on a last-minute whim, throw a blanket into my backpack. "Sorry, Katie. We didn't prepare for weather. We need to be careful." Disappointment clouds her features, though she doesn't plead or demand. "But we can try," I offer, unable to hold my flimsy resolve against her sad elfin face. "Let's see how we do."

"Yay!" Katie speeds ahead. We're in for a long afternoon; she should resist these adrenaline spurts and pace herself. Still, as she pushes on, I start to wonder if I have a new hiking partner.

"Hey, you're good at this," I tell her. "I miss hiking. Your dad used to be my hiking buddy, until he hurt his foot. He and I haven't been to the top of a mountain in years." I have a prairie girl's attitude to the landscape. The rocky peaks and dense forests inspire pure devotional awe. Driving out of the flatlands, as soon as I hit the foothills, I play one sentence on repeat: "Look at the mountains! Look at the mountains! Look at the mountains!" *Yes, Angie, we all see the mountains.* But for all my alpine enthusiasm, when I drive the opposite direction, out of the Rockies onto the prairie, I feel my shoulders drop, my neck release. I relax in the flatlands. Maybe that comfort alone is enough to explain the appeal of hiking: I need to get to a summit to find my natural environment — just me in the sky.

Katie and I count switchbacks as we go, betting on how many we'll take before we reach the bench. I can tell by the scenery that we'll pop out at the viewpoint on an even number. I guess twelve, while Katie votes for eight. We're at sixteen when we emerge, and I expect Katie to slow, but she only allows her butt to light on the seat for one photo before flittering up and toward the top. She ignores my reservations about the darkening sky and races heavenward. We haven't seen another human being in hours, and I remember what I love most about hiking: the way civilization falls away, the triviality of everyday society exposed. In this vast expanse of nature, I see our own lives in new proportions, my forty-some years against the mountains' three hundred million.

The peacefulness of this hike strikes me as new, not yet comfortable. It's the first time Katie and I have climbed a mountain alone together, and she's so much quieter than her brother. I try to prod her into conversation. "Excited about grade four?" "What was your favorite part of summer?" "Do you like the book you've been reading?" But her brief answers ("kinda," "camp," "yep") don't encourage me. Each of her responses puts a full-stop to our exchange. Eventually I concede that she prefers the silence. When Ollie and I walk, we blather about books, movies, story ideas. Katie is like her dad. When they walk, they walk. There's something insular and self-contained about them, qualities I don't understand. Ollie and I are more likely to spill out over everything, a mad jumble of uncontained words.

In the long stretches of quiet, my memory spits up a random object: a wedding gift Marty and I received years ago, a round mirror made of a window in a boat, a ship's porthole. Marty and I didn't have an actual wedding, but months after our elopement to Jamaica, we threw a party in our backyard. There were no invitations, just a few kegs of beer, a roasted pig, some music, and a Slip 'N Slide. No presents. Everyone welcome. An old friend named Brian showed up with the mirror as a gift, surprising me. Brian, a classic ski bum, had been part of our mountain town for as long as I could remember, maybe as long as anyone could remember. Recently, he would sometimes escape south during the winter, posting pictures on Facebook from various beaches, margarita in hand, grey chest hair exposed, face happy. His life seemed one long holiday, and I'd never known him to have a wife. On the back of the mirror, he wrote:

Marty + Angie:

Congratulations!!!

May the rest of your life be the best of your life.

xxx

Brian.

The sweetness of the gift, the romance of the gesture, toppled my idea of him. I guess I expected Brian to be more of a cynic about relationships. Marty and I hung the mirror in our first two homes, but the gift hadn't yet made its way to a wall in our third home when our marriage sank into the Dark Years.

Last winter, as we started to claw our way out of that gloom, I told Marty about a theory that love is essentially narcissistic. We fall in love with the positive reflection of ourselves in another's eyes. That positive reinforcement comes at its strongest during the start of a relationship, but as the years wear on, we start to see a less flattering reflection. Where I once looked in Marty's eyes and saw myself as smart and strong and sexy and fun, after kids I looked to the same place and saw myself as demanding, inadequate, dull, old, tired. This is what people call "falling out of love."

"We've been together a long time," I said. "Hopefully we'll be together for a lot longer. We're going to see different versions of each other. Sometimes the shifts can be so extreme it's almost like being married to a whole new person. But if we're open to the change and see each 'Marty' and each 'Angie' as a part in the whole of our story, we can enjoy the new changes injected into an old relationship."

"Well, I'll tell you what," Marty said. "I was sure happy to see the ass end of that last Angie." We laughed at his joke, ending our conversation. He didn't have a lot to say about the narcissistic nature of love and the role of reflection, but he often does not have a lot to say. Whenever I push for more access to his inner life, he says with a deprecating grin: "I like to have my internal thoughts internally." I'm not sure if he means the comment to make fun of me or himself.

When I went to bed that night, I saw Brian's mirror on my pillow, the reflective surface covered with bright red writing (*beautiful, hilarious, intelligent, caring, adventurous, strong . . .*). The adjectives spiraled around to a tight circle in the middle, the writing getting smaller and smaller as if Marty couldn't fit all the words he wanted. When he came to bed, I gestured to the mirror, still propped next to me on my pillow. For once, I couldn't think of anything to say.

A smile flickered, but he cast his eyes to his feet, shy. "That's what I see when I look at you," he said. "That's what I still see now." He lifted the mirror to my nightstand and put his head on the pillow next to mine. "I wrote the words in dry erase ink, so we can erase them and fill in others. To show the way we see each other. Like you said."

After making it through the Dark Years, Marty and I both try to be more aware, as much as we can, of the reflection we hold up for each other. It helps.

I suspect the same holds true for kids. We can reflect their images in ways that buoy them or ways that sink them. If there is no escaping language, if narrative is inevitable, we can at least be aware of how we shape it. We can tell stories in ways that make our days better and our lives happier.

In *Psychology Today*, Dr. Lisa Firestone sets out a number of ways a parent might inadvertently shape a child's self-story. If I am too critical of my daughter, she will internalize that negative voice and have poor self-perception, but if I praise my daughter too much and unrealistically, she will recognize the discrepancy between my story and her reality and will see herself as insufficient. Even the way a mother sees herself will influence a child's self-perception. If I talk constantly about needing to lose weight or being bad with money or failing to achieve certain goals, my children will learn to copy me and will continually find fault with themselves. With so many ways to mess up, what does Dr. Lisa Firestone recommend? Recognize the impossibility of perfection. Be reflective. Apologize for mistakes. Be honest, open, and mindful with children in order to create an environment where they can move forward independently with confidence and resilience.

As the trail gets more exposed, Katie's enthusiasm bubbles. She's still silent, but the determination and excitement vibrate in the set of her shoulders, the intensity in her eyes. She keeps her strides long and strong, her pace vigorous.

"Do not fall," I warn her. "If you fall, you will die." I look at the steep drop-off to our left and imagine her losing her footing, careening down the mountainside. Would she really die? Maybe not. Still. Falling here is not an option. "Keep your eyes on the trail. One careful step at a time."

Seeing her approach the peak, measured and calculated, but also daring and bold, I recognize the limitations of these dualities we depend upon, the ease with which we fall into them, pretending they make sense of our lives and our people. We draw on simple binaries like good/bad, shy/brave, happy/sad in an impossible attempt to impose order on chaos, to beat the ever-shifting complexity of life into manageable containers. I do it with almost everything. Katie: shy versus brave. My marriage with Marty: the dark years before versus the happy years now. My relationship with Gyllie: the wise elder friend versus the younger hopeless friend. Ollie and Katie: sound versus silence. I do take comfort in the tidiness of these sharp distinctions, all of us controlled and in our places, but that fixed clarity has little to do with our real lives, a series of unique stand-alone moments.

"Katie! Look! I can see the top!" I feel pulled to articulate what Katie will not. I need to make some noise, to hear the thrill of our experience vibrate in air. I hold my arms above my head and declare: *"I love it!"*

"Why did you quit hiking then?" She doesn't look back over her shoulder, just asks the question to the trail.

"Your dad and I did it together. I guess I was afraid to go out on my own when he couldn't come anymore. I don't have the best sense of direction. He always got all our gear and food ready and led the way." Despite seeing half a dozen doctors, Marty hasn't gotten a clear diagnosis on his foot pain. With no cure, he's simply cut back on mountain sports, one activity at a time. First he quit trail running and then he quit hiking. He still does his true loves — mountain biking and downhill skiing — but stops every twenty minutes to wrench his swollen, aching foot out of his boot. Each time, I see the knife-sharp pain in his face. Perhaps a challenge as basic as a sore foot contributed to our near-marital-death experience. In the complex tally of a happy marriage, what's the cost of a gradual decline in shared passions?

I slow Katie down occasionally to emphasize how high we've come, our town a tiny Lego village far below us. "We're looking down at clouds! We've walked into the sky." I'm reminded of another reason I love hiking: the simplicity of a goal achieved by one single determined step after another. On top of a mountain, I know I have accomplished exactly what I set out to accomplish. Though when Marty used to come out, he always reminded us not to let our enthusiasm run away at the top. "The summit is only halfway: you still have to get down. *Or die.*"

"Are you getting cold, K? Sorry, I should be better prepared."

The black clouds, looming nearby now, hold my gaze. The wind howls over the peak. Blue's big ears blow flat against his head.

"Mom! Stop! I'm fine." Katie doesn't slow her pace.

We should turn back, maybe. That would be the practical, responsible thing to do. But we're so close, and she's worked hard. Do I want her to come all this way and not make it? And really — irrational fears aside — what's the worst likely to happen? We could get caught in some rain or even a lightning storm. But I do have a blanket. We could take shelter under a tree and wait it out. If things go as badly as they could, we'd get home wet and hungry, maybe in the dusk. We're not going to get really hurt. We're certainly not going to die.

In an *Outside* magazine article, professional climber Will Gadd says it's never too early to teach children about risk management. As a father, he aims to build competence in order to increase confidence, but also to create autonomous individuals with critical thinking skills to make their own decisions. He takes his daughters out every weekend so they will learn how to assess danger in wilderness and in mountain sports. He emphasizes that his goal is not to eliminate risk — impossible both in mountain adventure *and in the rest of life* — but to recognize hazards, take precautions, and know when to bail. Today, Katie and I remain at a good distance from real danger.

If I'm not truly worried about our safety, what nags at me? What makes me feel like a bad parent for forging on, despite the black clouds?

I can already hear what people would say. That's what.

What kind of mother is she?

Who takes a child up a mountain in a lightning storm?

That's it: the fear of being judged.

"Mom, c'mon!"

Sinead, a current writing student of mine, recently completed a thesis on risky play. She started her own outdoor school based on what she learned from the research. The basic premise? Don't hover over children. Don't over-assist them. Unaided, kids will stretch as far as they're comfortable stretching. If they overreach, they might hurt themselves, and then they will learn about consequences and stay in safer territory next time. Katie looks more than comfortable. She vibrates with excitement, her determination to reach the summit infectious. One last time, I stare down the black clouds and banish the imagined headlines. Risk and play experts like Steve Smith and Joe Frost emphasize that the first step in building resiliency is teaching children to recognize hazards and evaluate severity. In looking at the clouds, assessing the contents of my backpack, and imaging worst-case scenarios, Katie and I do exactly as Smith and Frost suggest. If we end up wet and cold, both of us will come to the mountain better prepared next time.

As we close in on the peak, I worry more about Blue than I do about Katie. I tell her to stand back, and I push Blue's rump up the rocks while his front paws cling to the steep slope. Once I get him steadied on the cliff above us, I plead with him to stay put. A skittish dog bolting underfoot here truly could end in disaster. Katie has waited her turn, but she sparkles as she attacks the rocky slope. "She's unaided," I remind myself, "evaluating hazards, working to her own comfort level, taking risks, learning consequences — all as Gadd and Smith and Frost advise." I'm standing still, but my heart beats as if I'm sprinting. Goosebumps form on my arms. What about *my* comfort level?

"Are you sure you're okay doing this?"

"Mom! Yes!"

"Are you sure you're sure?"

"Mom. I am sure I'm sure." I love the confident edge in her voice. She thinks she doesn't need me. She's sure she's sure.

"Watch where you put each foot. Each handhold. Make sure you're secure. Get steady and safe before you move to the next." I yell nervous instructions at her. "Be slow. Be safe." *Don't fall. Don't fall. Don't fall. God. Do not fall.*

But I'm as proud as I am scared. I want a picture of her just like this: gripping the mountain, eyes hard and serious, her strong body outlined against the fierce sky, our home a mere spec far below. I stand firm, ready to catch her or at least break a fall. I don't dare let go of my focus on her, even for the brief moment it would take to get a photograph. I will, though, never forget the image: nine-year-old Katie, high above the world, rising up out of the mountain, godlike — divine, not because she's conquered nature, but because she's at one with nature, hands on rocks, feet in rubble, absorbed in the ascent, senses fully attuned to her natural environment.

Once she pops over the edge and emerges at the top, solid on her feet, I scramble up behind her. She stands under a sign aptly engraved with the words "Windy Pass." I brace myself against the rush of cold air. Oblivious to the discomfort, Katie lets a rare full smile spread across her freckled face. I extend my hand. I always initiate the shake, but she knows exactly what I mean and puts her palm against mine with no hesitation, and our voices synchronize.

"Where there's Smoke, there's Fire. Where there's Fire, there's Smoke." Clasp, clasp, punch, flutter.

"Am I the bravest girl you know?" The cheeky tilt of Katie's head makes me want to holler in delight. The cocky sheen to her eyes. *It's you.*

"The *freckliest* girl I know, for sure for sure." I tousle her hair. "You did it!"

She smiles and nods, looking taller, shoulders pulled back. The sky has started to spit and the wind roars hard, whipping our hair into our faces, but Katie's self-confidence fills me with buzzing warmth. "No," she says. I can see a joke bubbling in her eyes, tickling the corners of her mouth. "We're only halfway. We still have to get down. *Or die.*" The "or die" comes out grotesquely exaggerated, like the trailer for a bad horror movie, and my girl laughs, filled with joy. Light Katie, Happy Katie, she expands my heart.

"You climbed a whole mountain! How can a girl who climbs a mountain be afraid to go to the school office alone? People who climb mountains aren't shy." I'm not supposed to say the word. I catch myself too late, but I also hear Gyllie's laughing advice: *Say shy, don't say shy, whatever, just hug her, just love her.* "I'm so proud of you, Katie. You strong, confident, magnificent girl." I cannot know what Katie sees reflected in my eyes and how it makes her feel about herself, but I say a silent prayer that she will, at least sometimes, believe in the Katie of my heart.

The descent is fast and effortless, for one of us. Katie runs down the mountain. "Let's play tag," she shouts over her shoulder.

Play tag? On a mountain? This nine-year-old is going to get me killed. "How about I Spy with My Little Eye? I spy with my little eye something that is green."

"Mom! It's all green: it's forest." Her voice echoes up at me as she rails around the corner of another switchback.

Blue likes Katie's speed, but my old knees can't keep up. "Make noise," I yell after them. "Remember! Bears!"

By the time we get back to the car, the sky is a jubilant blue, not even a hint of the storm that nearly derailed us. Katie extends her hand first. I meet it and let her lead, her voice strong. "Where there's Smoke, there's Fire. Where there's Fire, there's Smoke." Clasp, clasp, punch, flutter.

"Hey, what do you think about next summer you and me make a hiking goal? A peak a week?" I've been dwelling on the end of summer during our descent, wondering how to carry this buzz into 2019.

She's pumped up on her first summit success, quick to nod her agreement.

"You know how I made a book about Ollie, about a year in his hockey life? What do you think of a book about our hiking season?"

Since the publication of *Home Ice*, many people have challenged me on the ethics of writing about my kids. The book mostly shared research about the cost of organized sports (on families, on relationships, on childhood, on bodies, on time, on pocketbooks); it presented the argument that contemporary families push kids toward excellence at too young an age, with the result that many young athletes lose the enjoyment, burn out, and quit by the age of thirteen. I turned my own family into the key characters, sharing the story of our relationship to organized sports, to personalize the research. People's objections have made me question my writing about Ollie and Katie. How much right do I have to tell the stories of their lives? What will they think when they're older? Is my book an invasion of their privacy? This kind of hand-wringing seems a defining feature of my generation. A writing mentor a generation older than me, Marni Jackson, author of *The Mother Zone*, says simply: "I wrote about my son until he grew up. Then he asked me not to write about him anymore, and then I stopped writing about him." She shrugs, easy.

In my home, among the only people whose opinions truly matter, concern attaches itself less to ethics of storytelling and more to an intent focus on keeping score. *Ollie got a book about him; when do I get a book, about me?*

"Would you like that?" I ask Katie now, "for our book to be a hiking book?"

She nods, and again that word comes to mind: resolute. But here the resolution is less somber, more joyful. "A book about you and me," she agrees with one hard nod. I see the thrill of the idea ignite. I don't know if my heart can take *two* full, wide Katie smiles in a single day.

"Uh-huh. A book about nature and kids, girls and confidence, lessons from hiking, mother and daughter relationships." I don't say a book about wildfire, about getting off screens, about prioritizing recreational time over organized sports, about our increasing disconnectedness from the wild, about how to talk to children about climate change. "About you and me, setting goals, getting outside." Already I'm thinking about the themes I'll put in play, the research I'll include. I'm not Knausgaard: I can't open a window on my life and call it a book. I need to build a bridge from my life to the lives of readers. I need to legitimize the personal sharing with expert research. *Well, you're not a man,* my inner-Gyllie says. *I don't see anyone beating down the door to publish* Her Struggle.

Or: *Portrait of the Artist as a Middle-Aged Mother Who Really Likes to Hike.*

My book thoughts have — as they too often do — pulled me away from my daughter. She's moved on, her focus shifting to post-hike ice cream. "Yes, sweet Katie. I will write a book about *you,* my strong and confident girl. My mountain-climber. My sometimes-brave, sometimes-shy Katie."

Three

The Forest, the Cyberverse, and Other Real Places

Let's not pretend that kids' personalities form while they're tucked under a bell jar, safely sealed, immune to their parents' problems and stresses. How did my life look during those years that Katie's demeanor appeared to shift? What did mine and Marty's preoccupations bring to her living environment? Katie spent ages eight and nine, a time critical to her growth and flourishment, submerged in a toxic soup of stress.

Not only had our marriage hit a ten on the conflict scale, but my work had consisted of two years of back-to-back controversies. First, I wrote a novel with two Ktunaxa characters, and some readers questioned my right, as a non-Indigenous writer, to do so. The more I tried to explain my perspective, the more I managed to anger my critics. I stepped away from my screen and spent my days with my best Ktunaxa friend, Anna. We walked the wilderness in her territory and drank tea in her cabin. She told me what she loved about my book and respected about my attempts at consultation with her Nation. In our long conversations, I came to better understand the politics of my situation.

Then I returned to my computer to discover the narrative of Evil Angie had continued to grow without my participation. The internet didn't need me for this conversation about me. A jarring disconnect emerged between my feet-on-the-ground life and my online life.

I would love to call the one life real and insist that the other is not real, or at least less so. But I have accumulated too many examples of the online world infecting real situations and real relationships. In the earliest days of this conflict, I traveled to the west coast to MC the retirement party of a festival director. Another woman in the industry, a soft-spoken and sweet woman with whom I'd only ever had pleasant interactions, approached me before the speeches started. I intuitively smiled and moved in to give her a hug. Her face froze in a grimace and she stepped out of my reach. "I came over only to let you know I'm here, for when it's my turn to speak," she said in the chilliest voice.

I saw the situation clearly then. This woman knew herself to be Good and on the side of Right, and she accepted the internet's recent declaration of me as Bad. She wanted no part of Bad. The internet had put me in a different world, marked me as a different kind of person. She and I never did have a single real-life conversation about my novel or about my version of what had happened. A collegial relationship ended. That is real.

Months into controversy, feeling under siege, I made a poor decision. The cyberverse responded to my mistake, fast and furious.

Friends and peers unfollowed me. People who didn't know me made hateful pronouncements on my character. Each time I looked online, the Twitter stream hit me with a full-force gush of hate.

Those with a stake in my career told me to stay offline. "Get off everything. Take some time away. Let the cyberbullying rage burn itself out."

But I couldn't. I, who had never taken a selfie in my life, started posting them daily. I cut off all my hair. I put pictures of myself on Instagram, Facebook, Twitter: shorn, ugly, repentant. I got urgent emails from professionals in a position to guide me: "We have already agreed you should stay off social media, yet you're still active on a number of platforms. We're worried about you." I don't know why I posted the pictures. Did I want my haters to know that they'd won, or think that seeing me so obviously miserable would appease them? Or did I need a new image to match a new me, a "me" I didn't yet recognize? Or did I put my picture on the Web simply to prove that, despite my shunning, I still existed? Perhaps to assure myself? *I am here.*

What do I tell my kids about their devices? I tell them, *Put that down! Get outside and play!* Neither Ollie nor Katie has an account on Facebook, Twitter, or Instagram, but both own iPads. Katie mostly uses hers for watching videos or FaceTiming friends. Ollie posts movie reviews on YouTube and plays a few games on Xbox. We worry about screen time and limit them to an hour a day, always prioritizing outdoor activity. Anything is better than a face glued to an iPad. Yet, here I was letting my life be ruled by a screen that fit in my palm, as if nothing existed beyond its five-by-two-and-a-half inches. Not only did I set the worst example, but my obsession with my own downfall got between me and the children.

Finally, I could no longer stand the wrath, and I did close my social media accounts. Stress-inspired cold sores covered my mouth. They ran together, bleeding into each other, until I couldn't count them anymore. My face pounded in pain, but I didn't go to the doctor. I lay on the couch in the fetal position with Blue snuggled warm by my chest. "Oh well. Blue loves me," I said to Marty, who hovered around, ensuring I ate and drank occasionally.

"He's a good dog. He knows you need him. He's not going anywhere."

"My One True Soul Mate."

When I talk about those weeks now, I always end by saying, "But I wasn't suicidal."

Marty gives me an assessing stare. "Weren't you?"

I do remember saying over and over again: "I'm dying I'm dying I'm dying I'm dying." It felt that way, as if a notion of me had perished.

A few friends checked in on me. One local man, a sixty-something ski bum who moved to Canada to take advantage of his dual citizenship when he needed open-heart surgery, called me every morning. "It's your daily mental health check. Hanging in there?"

"People will forget," he assured me each time. I didn't believe him. Something had ended. I didn't yet understand what.

When Marty came home from work those evenings, he found me right where he had left me at six a.m.: curled up on the couch, under my Grandma blanket, both arms around Blue. "Can you look?" I'd ask him. "For me. I can't. But I need to know if it's still happening. Go to Twitter, sign in through your account. Search Angie Abdou."

I watched him scroll and scroll and scroll. "Yep, it's still happening." He lifted his eyebrows and continued to scroll. "Wow. They really hate you." He placed his phone face down on the island and smiled, as if he could infect me with his sudden shift in mood. "Well, you wanted to be famous," he offered. "Now you're famous."

Eventually, I found the strength to reach out to the friends I wanted to maintain. I said sorry personally to the individual my mistake had hurt the most. Our exchange went better one-to-one, after we cut out the internet masses. I owed her an explanation, and I wanted her to know that I felt true remorse. But as I began to be able to see the situation with some clarity, I couldn't understand why everyone on the internet thought they needed to get in on that exchange, why they all felt so entitled to a piece of me.

In *So You've Been Publicly Shamed*, Jon Ronson shares stories of people's careers and personal relationships ruined based on one stupid tweet or unfortunate Facebook picture. Ronson's number one piece of advice comes as no surprise to me: do not engage. No apology will be enough. No explanation will suffice. Any attempt will only give the crowd more ammunition.

Stay silent.

Let them run out of material.

Hope they will forget.

Pray for someone else to slip up, do something stupid.

I followed Ronson's advice and ignored statements that seemed aimed at baiting me into a reply. I stuck close to Blue, who loved me.

When I think back on those winter months, I don't think of Ollie and Katie. I must have taken care of them — woken them in the morning, fed them breakfast, packed their bags, gotten them to school. I must have been there when they returned so I could manage snacks and after-school schedules. They must have been there to see me crying on the couch and Marty reading the reams of hate mail, sharing the highlights, my face an aching mess of open wounds. They might have caught me sitting on my bed, staring blankly out the window at the thick belt of trees that separated us from town, my head tilted up to the towering cottonwoods, my eyes and mind resting in the calming blur of trees. But I don't remember my children, can't imagine them into the scene even now. I must have stumbled through the rote parenting tasks in a zombie state.

A kind colleague e-mailed to suggest I take a mental health leave from our online university until the worst of the social media rage subsided, allowing me to cope better with regular life. He sent me links to research about the connection between cyber-mobbing and suicidal ideation. I did not take the leave (my many years as a long-distance competitive swimmer had conditioned me to muscle through pain), but I don't remember how I accomplished my teaching work in those early weeks. All I recall from that time? The couch, my Grandma blanket, the blur of cottonwoods, my One True Soul Mate Blue, and hate.

Every morning, upon waking, I would have a moment when I'd forgotten how my life had changed. But as I came to full consciousness, my new reality greeted me with a punch to the gut.

Instead of getting out of bed, I closed my eyes, trying to lose myself to sleep, unable to do it all again. I didn't want to start another day to learn who else had unfollowed, unfriended, and discredited me.

But one morning before I made that transition from ignorant bliss to knowing despair, an old-growth cottonwood out my bedroom window captured my attention. It stood high above the rest and beamed energy, its positivity flooding in like sunlight. Its branches reached out to me. While I remained in a semi-dream state, the massive tree embraced me with unconditional love. A warm calm flooded through my body. Enraptured, I gave myself over to the experience of the tree. The warmth and calm gradually morphed into a full-bodied euphoric high. I let the tree love me. The experience, true and real, lifted me. In my mind, I floated above the mattress, my gaze locked on the tree.

I had never felt so light, so enveloped in kindness.

I didn't tell anyone about this encounter, not right away. But I held a small bit of the kindness and love in my chest as I proceeded with my day. When the new, but already familiar, anxiety clawed at me, I raced to a window. My eyes found my cottonwood. I opened myself to its energy. I breathed.

In the following mornings, I learned to turn to the tree as I woke, ensuring it was the first thing I saw. The sensation of the tree got me through the winter, and I started to note patterns.

"I'm not going to have any wine," I told Marty one night in spring as the forest behind our house burst into vibrant green life. "I have this thing going on with the cottonwood. The big one outside our bedroom window. It's really kind to me. But I can't feel its kindness when I'm hungover. It works better if I stay sober."

"The tree?"

The room fell into an intense silence. Both Ollie and Katie turned to listen. I probably shouldn't have said anything. "Yeah, it's — well, you're atheist, so you might not understand, but I had a kind of religious experience. Mystical."

"With . . . the tree?"

"Yep."

"Okay." Marty turned to the kids, his eyebrows high. "The tree doesn't like it when mom drinks."

The tree became a joke around our house. "My dad's atheist," Ollie told his friend Harley. "I am too. But not my mom. My mom believes in The Tree."

"Really, Oliver," I said, refusing to be embarrassed. "An eleven-year-old atheist? You don't think that's a bit arrogant? To believe you have all the mysteries of the universe figured out in sixth grade?"

"Yeah, Ollie," Marty interjected, "you need to be almost fifty before the universe lets you in on the mystery of The Tree. Even I'm not old enough for that. Only mom is *that* wise."

Katie giggled covering her mouth with her hand.

"It couldn't be a cedar or a spruce?" Marty asked. "Your god has to come as a cottonwood, the weed of the forest?"

"Okay. Haha. Laugh if you want. I know what I know." But I spoke as if making fun of myself. Laughing was easiest. I sensed no mean spirit in their ribbing. The tree became a quick and easy joke, for all of us, at a time we needed laughter.

"Mom's having wine," Katie would chirp in her cheekiest voice. "Don't tell The Tree!"

"Maybe The Tree will suddenly fall over on her when she takes her first sip," Ollie laughed, "and then we'll know The Truth."

I learned to keep quiet about my tree, most of the time. Until Zachary, a novelist from Vancouver, visited. Novelists like weird ideas, they crave strange experiences — anything to challenge their beliefs, stretch their ways of thinking, provide material. The weirder, the better. Zach had focused his full attention on winning Blue's affection, refusing to be deterred by my dog's aloof personality. "He really is a stunning animal."

As long as Zach agreed with me about Blue's overwhelming beauty, I did not mind the diverted focus. "Cheese is the trick," I told him, passing over a big block of cheddar and a knife. "Blue will do anything for cheese."

Distracted, Zach talked to me while making small offerings to Blue — first setting a piece of cheese on the floor at arm's length, tempting Blue to come close, eventually holding a piece in his fingers, reaching toward Blue without making eye contact. "C'mon, sweet Blue," he muttered under his breath, hoping to lure him close enough for a pat. "We'll be friends before I leave, Mr. Blue." Blue, eyes on the cheese, took tentative steps toward Zach's fingers but then backed away, circling around to hide behind the kitchen island before coming into sniffing range again. "You're feeling better, though, hey? Recovered?" I knew Zach meant the question for me, but he didn't make eye contact, too focused on his project. Like Blue, I responded well to the averted gaze.

"Yeah. I had this thing with a tree. An . . . experience. It helped." I gestured over my shoulder toward the cottonwood out back, but Zach wasn't looking.

"A tree?" It was the same question Marty asked but without the trace of mockery. In Zach's tone, I heard only curiosity.

He stretched out his hand. "Cheese, Blue. All for you." He stared away from Blue toward the front door, ensuring he posed no threat.

Not sure at all that Zach was listening to me, I told him about the tree: its unconditional love, the overwhelming sense of security, the sudden confidence that I would be okay, that a force beyond my understanding was taking care of me. "It made me wonder about the medieval mystics," I said. "They were persecuted, pushed to despair, and then they had these almost erotic experiences of divine intervention. Maybe that's how our bodies protect us — when we feel attacked and driven to despair, the body floods us with some saving hormone, a natural antidepressant, a much-needed high."

"You," Zach said, "are working very hard to explain away an experience." Zach possessed a confidence I never will. He didn't hesitate to speak with certainty about the essentially unknowable. He didn't need to couch discussions of the divine in jokes and self-deprecation. "I was raised in the church," he said, as Blue tentatively took the piece of cheese from between his two fingers. "You don't need to explain any of it away to me."

My ongoing romance with the tree pulled me outdoors. I reopened my social media accounts, telling Marty, "Maybe I'll leave eventually, but I want to do so of my own accord. I don't want to be chased off."

Marty's anger surprised me. He'd supported me through the conflict, without question or reservation, but as the online animosity wound down, I saw his fatigue. "You're back on Twitter and Facebook 'to see how it goes'? You might as well stick your head in the outhouse to see if it still stinks."

Over dinner that night, I promised him I would keep social media in perspective, stay offline as much as I could. "I don't want to run away, Marty. I don't want to be scared."

I told him about Zoey Leigh Peterson, author of *Next Year for Sure*. She and I briefly toured together after the release of her novel. She went online then, as we must, to fulfill the obligations of a new author, but she spoke wistfully of the tour ending so she could put her iPhone back where it belonged: the bottom of her sock drawer. We can't, in the twenty-first century, eschew the online world, can't pretend it doesn't exist or that it's not real, but we can keep it in perspective, remind ourselves of its proper place. I think a lot about setting that example for my kids, who have never known a world that doesn't include the e-world. If adults can be so relentlessly cruel online, and so broken by that cruelty, imagine children.

Experts, though, surprise me by claiming social media is a game-changer for introverted kids, a lifesaver in the way it can help shy kids overcome personality barriers to excel in school. In *Psychology Today*, Susan Cain argues that teachers can use social media in the classroom to open students' minds and flatten hierarchies, to give the quiet kids a voice, and to diminish the boisterous kids' dominance. Her essay reminds me that online platforms are not inherently evil; they're tools that we can decide how to use. I need to manage my usage, if not to save myself, then at least to set an example for my socially vulnerable daughter. Moving my iPhone to the bottom of the sock drawer would serve as a good reminder of how much space and what significance I want to allot to virtual life. I told Marty all of this, and I promised him that I would henceforth put the social media world last in my list of priorities and ensure the good stuff came first: family, laughter, work, nature, exercise.

I grew to enjoy the company of trees more than people. For the first time in my life, I craved a break from words. I thought of an observation I once heard from novelist Barbara Gowdy. At a literary festival, an onstage interviewer asked her what she would write next. She answered that she didn't know if she wanted to write at all. She gestured to a narrow space in front of her face, a tight and claustrophobic square. She talked about living in that confined area during the writing of a book, nothing but her mind and the computer screen. "And then when you break away and look up, there's *the world*." She swept her arms in a grand, joyous gesture. She thought maybe she was ready to give up writing, she said, trade it in for *the world*.

Her words moved me, startled me, the idea that we must pick: Our Writing or The World. She got me thinking about what we sacrifice to pump out these books. Running outside had always been a crucial component of my own writing process. When in motion, my body set to a well-known meditative task, I freed my mind to work with the raw material I'd entered during a morning at the computer. My best dialogue, insights, characters all came to me while running on the trails.

But that winter, when I needed nature for its own merits, not as an engine to produce words, I realized how my writing process actually cut me off from the landscape, in exactly the way Gowdy described. I ran with my head down, shoulders hunched, turned inward to focus on the ideas inside my head instead of the beauty around me. That winter, I worked to change my habits. I drew myself outward and let my eyes settle on the mountains, the river, the trees. I pulled back my shoulders and puffed out my chest, exposing myself to the elements. I took full deep breaths, filled myself with the mountain air, let it open me. I left my gloves at home, wanting to experience the sensation of winter chill on bare skin. I took pleasure in the effort of running through the deep snow, bracing myself through the icy sections, always reminding myself to look up and out, not down and in.

"God, it's so beautiful," I said to Blue, who bounded at my side, never needing a leash. He disappeared burrowing through the deep hills of white. When he popped out of the drifts, fluffy snow crystals covered his face, brilliant diamonds against his jet-black fur, his aqua ice-eyes shining in the winter wonder, his face laughing. "We're lucky," I thought. "Here, in this wild, gorgeous world — so very lucky."

"We'll be okay, Blue."

And then I publish a new book.

Controversy hits again, this one local, but the modus operandi is the same. The conflict plays out on social media, and the people who most enthusiastically pile on show no sign of having read what I wrote. The day after I launch *Home Ice*, a man posts on Facebook insisting that I slammed the town and everyone in it. He cuts and pastes my paragraphs out of context, removing crucial filters and distorting the meaning of my words. He summons his followers to stand together against me. Before they have had a chance to read the book for themselves, they rally to his battle cry.

In a 2017 book called *Behave: The Biology of Humans at Our Best and Worst*, Robert Sapolsky explains the satisfaction inherent in punishing people for perceived violations of norms. When we torture a perceived evildoer, our bodies release dopamine, which stimulates the reward-related regions of the brain. Group outrage has the same neurological function. Participating in an attack, even a verbal one, excites us and invigorates our bodies. In terms of brain activity, an online mobbing pleases the participants in exactly the same way as an old-fashioned public stoning. Sapolsky explains that in the social media brand of torture, our reward is twofold because participants also receive positive social feedback — in the form of "likes," a growing "friend" count, and supportive comments — and they thus benefit from a created sense of belonging as well as the excitement of exclusion.

Understanding the psychology of online mobs does not make the mobbing any easier to bear.

I knew local readers might react negatively to my memoir. People, I have learned, do not like being written about. My hometown is a tourist destination, so we're used to having that marketing lens on our lives — *Come to our town! It's perfect! We're living the dream!* — but we're less accustomed to a literary lens.

My favorite writers whose books focus on the places in which they lived — Alice Munro, Margaret Laurence, Sharon Butala — all experienced shunning at home. One summer, after hearing Sharon Butala speak at the Saskatchewan Festival of Words, my mom said to her, "Some people where you live must not like you."

Butala responded, "Oh *nobody* likes me there."

Perhaps local rejection is an inescapable fate of the type of writer I strive to emulate.

Before the release of *Home Ice*, I had, in theory, braced myself against this possible response, drawing strength from the tradition of women writers I so admired. But the reality of rejection hits me harder than the theory. Butala's comment did not prepare me for the way it feels to walk down Main Street and have nobody smile at me, nobody say hello. With one Facebook post, I find myself back on a ride I didn't like the first time.

Why would anyone be a writer in the internet age?

People I don't even know post verbal abuse on my Facebook timeline, but I don't get sucked in like last year. Before I respond to anything, Blue and I head back into woods. With so much online noise coming from people in my own town, the thought of leaving the house fills me with anxiety. If they're so rude online, what will they do in person? I am afraid of the grocery store and the hockey rink, the public parks and Main Street, but I'm drawn to the forest. In public, people I've known for decades pretend not to see me. A friend of twenty years — one who spent the afternoon before her wedding getting her hair done in my kitchen while Marty, shirtless in a bowtie, served her and her bridesmaid Long Island iced tea — appears to participate in the Facebook pile on. When we meet to talk about her role, she says, "Yeah, you should move. I would."

People are unpredictable, the trees constant.

Away from the computer, I realize that the people who matter will read the book. I repeat my mantra: people do not get to have opinions about books they have not read. I will not defend a book to people who can't be bothered to open it.

I'm out. The internet loves a monster. This time the bullies can have the pile-on without me. Marty's right: I don't need to put my head back in the outhouse to know it still stinks.

I do my book tour. I focus on the real-life connections I make on the road. I post simple updates online, to meet the expectations on any writer with a new book. I get outside as much as I can. All goes well.

"Take the high road," Marty says.

"Trust me. I have a nosebleed up here."

"Perfect. Fuck 'em."

"Yep. Fuck 'em."

It's not the worst philosophy to live by.

But stepping away from the internet — away from social media — is an act we (and our children) have to choose daily. "Once and for all" does not work, not with the platforms so fatally woven into our lives. My first major slip happens while I'm at the Banff-Mineral Springs Hospital waiting for news on Marty. He finally got a diagnosis on his foot (Morton's neuroma) and an easy surgery to fix it, but then the foot became badly infected, resulting in an emergency surgery. The previous week, I had a spot on CTV's *The Social* talking about *Home Ice*. In reply to an innocuous CTV tweet with a link to my eleven-minute segment, a local hockey parent brings up the hometown controversy and calls me and my book garbage.

"New me" should ignore this. But the tweet comes through as I stand tired and hungry in a hospital hallway, worried about what's taking so long. I expected to have gotten the okay to take Marty home hours ago, and I put off eating dinner or finding a place for us to stay. It's very late, and I haven't received a clear update on his status. I'm stressed and perhaps more than a little "hangry." After two months of taking the high road — two months of staying largely silent — I lash out.

When Marty learns that I've engaged in the online conflict, he says only two words: "Angie. Don't."

"I know. I won't. I won't." I feign a smile. "I promise, I won't."

When I do slip and give Marty the daily death count — who snubbed me, who yelled at me, who unfriended me, who blocked me — he shrugs. "Why do you care?" He easily dismisses each slight. "So she blocked you. Does she know you?"

"No."

"Do you respect her?"

"No."

"What would you tell Katie if a bunch of girls at school were ganging up on her like this?"

"Ignore them. You're better than that."

"Do you care what they think?"

"Maybe." I don't tell Marty what I've learned from my research, that girls learn their social behaviors from their mothers. A mother who cares too much what people think will likely have a daughter who also fears social judgment.

"*Should* you care what they think?"

"No."

"Do they matter?"

"No."

"Who matters?"

"Just you guys."

"And do we love you?"

"Yes." I make myself smile. It's true: my family, they're the ones who really matter. And when I get away from my computer, away from the internet's mean over-simplifications and unambiguous vilifications, I can forget the rest. Outside, surrounded by awe-inspiring vistas, the raging river, the fragrant forest, I can even forget myself and my own small squabbles. Running the trails, with my heart pounding, my senses alert, and my feet solid on the dirt, none of the online conflict matters.

I wonder if I enter the forest to chase the high of my euphoric experience with the cottonwood. Do I hope that trees might really offer divine assistance, spiritual transcendence, comfort, and answers? I decide it's okay if I do. At fifty, I have spent much of my life chasing highs offered by social media's external affirmations or the euphoria of alcohol or drugs or men. No harm can come of a tree.

Maybe this forest world is no more real than the online world — maybe less in terms of the impact it can have on my professional life or even on how I am perceived in my own community — but I want to keep the forest at the forefront as an antidote to the online world. I need to remember which of those worlds belongs at the bottom of my sock drawer. Hopefully that prioritization will rub off on my kids as they learn to navigate their way. I will always ask them: How does engaging in that e-space make you feel? What draws you to it? What's your mood when you get off? Does that social media platform make your life better or worse? If worse, then find a more effective way to manage the tool or, if necessary, know when to drop it altogether.

With Ollie and Katie in bed, Marty and I put on some music and sit on our worn leather couch, ignoring the stuffing popping out of its seams, and share the details of our day. I tell him about the new alertness I've brought to my trail running, how I look up, take it all in, absorb *the world*. "People can hate me," I say. "They can make my life here uncomfortable. But they can't take this away from me." I gesture toward the back window at our cottonwood forest, the shadowy Lizard Range, the ball of moon over Mount Fernie. "*This* is my Fernie. The mountains, the river, the trees."

Liquid rises in Marty's eyes when I say "my Fernie." We've had a tough few years. He pops out his bottom lip, mocking his own rush of emotion, but he doesn't wipe his eyes, doesn't drop my gaze. "I've never heard you say that before," he says. "*My Fernie.* I like it. I always think you want to leave."

"No. I just needed to find the part of Fernie that works for me."

I reach into his lap to hold his hand, and I think about the coming summer. Mine and Katie's peak-a-week challenge is almost here. I will make up for losing myself again to the online drama; I will bounce back from this season of absence. I cannot wait to introduce Katie to *my Fernie*, to let her in on its secret and the profound depth of solace that any of us can find there, if we look. I promise myself that I will always choose the weeds of the forest over the weeds of the internet. I hope my daughter does too.

Four

Wander to Wonder

"The ground is dry. The rivers are dry. It's all fucking dry."
At the table next to us, four men, a collage of flannel and denim, take up a lot of room. Big bodies, big voices, big boots. They fill the claustrophobically tiny coffee shop. We're not eavesdropping exactly, but we can't help letting their conversation envelop us. They're either oblivious to my little family sitting within reaching distance, or they're performing for us. They refuse to tilt their gaze our way, never breaking the fourth wall. Ollie and Katie stare as if these lumberjacks are part of the local scenery that we've traveled far to see.

"Jack had to blow yesterday morning." The man closest to us stretches out his legs as he talks, drops his heavy heel onto the floor, shaking the small room.

"That couldn't have gone well for him," his buddy answers, taking the last empty seat and waving to the waitress for a coffee. "He was pretty lunched the night before."

"Yep. He had a full-throttle drunkover."

"Drunkover!" All five of them laugh. "Fuck. Been there."

Ollie and Katie catch our eyes at the swear word, as if they're getting away with something just by hearing the curse. Marty and I nod them off with a don't-say-anything stare.

"Eat your eggs," I whisper. We've all got a fried egg on an English muffin. We didn't see the full menu until after we ordered so believed this option, written on a sticky note at the till, to be our only choice. The woman serving breakfast didn't let on otherwise. "We'll have four."

"What time is it anyways? No early-bird start today." The guy with the stretched-out legs lifts his ball cap as he talks, scratches his scalp, puts the cap back on. "You're all late. I thought I was going to have to solve the world's problems myself."

"Well that would be a challenge." The men laugh again, slouched in their chairs. Their conversation could take place anywhere. I'm reminded of my dad and his six coffee buddies who for decades had met every morning in Moose Jaw, Saskatchewan, swapping stories about weather, drinking, politics, and sports. But this morning we're in Port Renfrew, British Columbia.

A sign on the front door says "Tofino's That Way," pointing the direction to the trendy surf town with a clearly extended middle finger. Being from a tourist destination ourselves, we're familiar with the joke and know ourselves to be the target of this one. Squamish, less than an hour from Canada's most famous skiing mecca, has the same sign: "Whistler's That Way." *Fuck off, tourist,* that's the sign's message, *no five-star service here.* And also, *We like our home the way it's always been: without you.*

Tourism alters a place, and not all locals welcome the change. The influx of visitors sets off a proprietary instinct: *this* belongs to *us.* The locals have rights to a place; the tourists do not. In my experience, where people draw the line to divide local from tourist has everything to do with when they themselves arrived. For some, a person has to be fourth generation to qualify as a Fernie local. For others, spending a single full ski season makes one worthy of local status. We all want to close the door right after we arrived — I'm a local, but anyone who came after me? Only a tourist. In a single day of travel, my family has moved from the local side of that equation to the tourist side, and the transition is a bit jarring. We tread carefully.

This Port Renfrew coffee shop, making its point loud and clear, has the "Tofino's That Way" sign on both sides of the door, in and out, meaning that the middle finger points in opposite directions. "Well then," Marty leans over and whispers, though the effort seems unnecessary since nobody's paying any attention to us. "Which way *is* Tofino?" He points one middle finger to the right of him and the other to the left. "This way or that way?"

"Shhhh!!!" I'm laughing, but the signs don't lead me to expect the locals to be in a particularly good humor, at least not when it comes to us. They're saving their laughs for Jack and his drunkover.

Today we're starting the Juan de Fuca Marine Trail, a reportedly beautiful forty-seven-kilometer hike along the west coast of Canada's Vancouver Island, just south of the more famous West

Coast Trail. The Juan de Fuca runs from near Port Renfrew, close enough we can hike right from town, to Sooke (just outside of Victoria, the province's capital). With the kids in tow, we expect the expedition might take up to seven days. We pulled Ollie and Katie out of school so we could be here in early June before the crowds arrive. With a bit of luck, we'll hardly see another soul.

We planned every logistical detail, except a place to stay last night. I guess we did, in fact, expect Port Renfrew to be more like Tofino. Instead, we arrived, tired and hungry, to discover no cell service, minimal lodging, and only two places to eat, one a loud bar that Ollie refused to set foot in and the other a food truck attached to a temporary building at the end of a pier. We ate burgers, watched eagles fishing, and inquired about where we could find some beds for the evening.

"What's the population here?" I asked the server, who was friendly enough but also cashing out and keen for us to be on our way. She put down a stack of fives and picked up the tens before looking our way.

"You mean in the summer or in the winter?" She tucked her hair behind her ear, the wad of ten-dollar bills firm in her other hand.

"Let's say right now-ish."

"One hundred and eighty." She licked her thumb and resumed her counting.

Not Tofino.

The waitress told us about a friend who rented a bedroom above his garage. "It's just up the road." Luck turned our way and we got hold of him and found the space un-booked, though Ollie declared himself too old to share a bed with his sister and started his camping trip a night early, sleeping on the floor in his tenting gear.

We'd left Fernie the day before in smoke so thick we couldn't see the mountains. A cousin texted that he might come visit for the weekend because he had to get out of the apocalyptic doom in Calgary. I wrote him back, warning we were suffocating in Fernie too.

It can't be as bad as here, he responded.

Sorry, I wrote, attaching a photo out our living room windows, a view of nothing but grey, *it is that bad*.

He stayed home.

In Fernie, we'd gotten used to forest fires dominating the summer season. Breathing in the toxic air, suffering burning eyes, being unable to see across the street, our bodies always racing with anxiety as if in a permanent state of crisis — that had become normal fare for July and August. But May? Smoke in May had everyone talking. What on Earth would we be in for by August?

On our arrival in Port Renfrew, the air felt crisp and clean against my travel-weary face. Right out of the truck, I could smell the cedars and taste the sea. Katie leapt from the backseat to the ground, stretching her hands far above her head with a giant breath. "Wow," she said simply, sniffing again and turning her sleepy blue eyes to the dark water.

Despite the delicious air, the view wasn't clear, and not only because we'd arrived at dusk. At the water's edge, the small buildings sat buried in thick grey, a haze I knew well. I resigned myself to a week of hiking in the fall-out of raging forest fires.

"It's smoky here," I said to the man renting us a room, only to make conversation. "It's early for smoke."

"It's not smoke," he said. "It's fog. We're on the ocean. We get fog." He might as well have added *you dumb tourist.*

"Ah, gotcha. It was smoky where we live, yesterday when we left, really smoky. That's why I . . ." Never mind.

This coolness from a stranger didn't bother me. The drama accompanying the release of my hockey book had died down, but I still walked around town with my shoulders at my ears, alertness bordering on paranoia, never knowing when I'd get a cold shoulder or a public takedown. I made light of the high school behavior, claiming, "The pretty girls don't like me anymore, but the artsy kids still hang out with me." I could laugh at being ostracized, but the local shunning stung. This Port Renfrew man's coolness didn't sting.

I smiled and took the keys from our host and dropped the conversation, eager to get to sleep if only to speed up the time until tomorrow's escape into wilderness.

My original 2019 summer hiking plan hadn't involved a trek down the Juan de Fuca Trail. But Marty stepped in. He had felt sidelined during the winter as Katie and I chattered about our peak-a-week challenge. Our enthusiasm combined with his freshly repaired foot got him fired up, and by midwinter he'd made a serious pastime of googling "epic family trails." He suggested Katie and I launch our hiking season with our first family backpacking adventure.

But I wanted a mother-daughter adventure — that's where the whole idea originated. Could I say that? To insist that I wanted to share this time only with Katie would be to deliberately exclude my son and my husband.

"The idea was to hike local," I said instead. "You know, low impact. We don't have to get on a plane — or even in a car — to take a holiday from our lives. We're surrounded in every direction by these spectacular mountains. Even if we tried, we couldn't get to the top of all of them in a single summer. Why travel?"

"Look, though!" Marty pushed his iPhone toward my face, waving panoramic photographs of coastal views. "We're in a sweet spot: kids old enough, us not too old. We've been wanting to do a trip like this."

"I know you, Marty." I felt the familiar heart grip of stress. "A backpacking trip will be an excuse to buy shit. I like hiking because we don't need all that stuff. Walking in the mountains: shoes and water. It's simple." I recognized the smirk on Marty's face. "What? Oh, Marty. You've *already* bought stuff, haven't you?" We'd hit a sore spot. Money always spawned discord in our marriage.

I hate buying stuff. Marty lives for buying stuff.

"Well, maybe a new hammock tent," Marty admitted. "We needed one."

"Needed?"

"And packs for Ollie and Katie, now that they're big enough to carry their own. And they'll need new hiking boots."

"Marty." This old conversation sucked the energy right out of me. I didn't want to tally up the grand total for tents and boots and packs. Every little bit of new gear would be the best too because Marty only ever bought the best. He hadn't discussed any of the purchases with me because he already knew what I thought.

My objections loaded quickly, ready to aim and fire. But recently, Marty and I had both learned to back away from a fight. I kept my voice neutral, my face neutral, my words neutral. I didn't ask, *How much money?* I didn't say, *We never talked about this.* I didn't say, *You spend money like a drunk billionaire.*

"And just one more . . ." Marty smiled. He must've figured me to be in a good mood and decided to unleash all his spending news at once. "I've got a plan for a new sleeping system, so we can snuggle. We can't cuddle in our gear now, with our separate bags and Therm-a-Rests. So I ordered a double system, with better padding for our old backs. It'll be more comfortable."

I tried to let myself be won over by his snuggling motivation. For two years, since Katie learned about need-versus-want in her second-grade social studies class, I'd been drawing on the distinction to get Marty and me to think about the environmental impacts of consumerism in our own adult lives. The lesson had not caught on. "But we don't really *need* any of it, Marty. That's what I like about hiking: how little we actually need."

"Yes!" Marty's face lit up, an addict catching a glimpse of his favorite drug. "Light hiking! That's a whole thing too! I can buy you stuff for that: ultralight pack, ultralight sleeping bag, ultralight sleep pad, ultralight stove."

"Gearhead." I chose to laugh. "Please don't. Don't buy me anything."

I objected to Marty's takeover partly on environmental grounds, my desire to be less obnoxious consumers and polluters. But I also put up resistance simply at the idea of him moving in on *my* hiking plan. My alone time with my daughter. Marty and I have always both been control freaks and we historically solved the clash — the impossibility of us *both* being in control — by avoiding teamwork altogether. I had gone one way with Ollie and Marty, the other with Katie.

With my "Summer of Mommy and Katie," my "Peak a Week," my "Smoke and Fire," I had simply reversed our old mistake instead of changing it: I grabbed Katie and left Marty with Ollie. Marty was right. He and I needed to find ways of working as a parenting team, so all four of us could spend time together. I could try to be less controlling. It was his money. If he was dying to spend it, maybe I needed to let him. I recognized long ago I'd never win the war for frugality, not with Marty. "Okay," I finally said. "I hope you really love your job."

"So that's a yes? To Juan de Fuca?"

"Sure. Let's do it."

"Okay. Here it goes." I hold up my iPhone so Ollie and Katie can see the screen from the backseat. "I'm turning it off! I'm turning it all the way off and putting it away. For a whole week."

"Yeesh, mom," Katie says. I can hear the eye roll. "Drama much?"

"You could take it," Marty says, slipping his truck into a spot where it should sit in shade for most of the week. "We probably won't have cell service anyway. You could mostly power down, but use it for pictures."

"Mom without an iPhone?" Ollie sounds too much like a teenager for my liking. "I'll believe it when I see it."

"Seriously. I'm going cold turkey. Just you watch. If I can't do it here, I can't do it anywhere." Mount Sinai School of Medicine defines addiction as "a brain disorder characterized by compulsive engagement in rewarding stimuli despite adverse consequences." I talk about my iPhone like an addict talks about booze or drugs, for good reason. I catch myself reaching for it without thinking, the way a nicotine addict reaches for the pack of cigarettes. During public events, I sneak off to the bathroom with my phone so I can have a furtive peek at the activity on my social media feeds, the way an alcoholic sneaks off for a hit of booze. I'm embarrassed when someone catches me flicking to Facebook in a crowd, as ashamed as if I'd been caught with a spot of powder under my nose. I know all these emotions and behaviors associated with my iPhone — the obsession, the mindless devotion, the relentless compulsions, the deviousness, the embarrassment, the shame, the remorse. I know the cycle well, and it feels exactly like addiction. "Ta-dah!" I slam my iPhone into the glove box.

We have to walk two kilometers up a paved road to start the hike at the Botanical Beach trailhead. Marty gets the kids all loaded up under their new backpacks. I stare at Katie. "Oh my god, are you sure, Marty? She looks so tiny. Can you carry that, Katie, sweetie?" Katie is a stick figure under her giant new pack. "You're going to do forty-seven kilometers carrying that load?"

Never one to say no, Katie nods her freckly face and grabs her straps, standing up taller and stronger. "Totally. I can. Easy." Her hair looks gorgeous, the auburn glinting in the morning sunlight. Though the forecast has promised rain, we've woken to a stunning, perfect day. The sun has burned off the haze from last night, and golden rays filter through the cedar forest.

"You're amazing," I tell my daughter, but I give Marty a quick look, one that says *Really? Are you sure?* We forget she's only ten. We ask a lot of a ten-year-old.

"What about me?" Ollie grumps. "What about my pack?"

"You two! Not everything is a contest." I recognize my hypocrisy — and how much of their behavior they learn from us. "Yes, Ollie, you're amazing too."

"Their packs are light," Marty says, hauling his own out of the truck bed with a loud clunk. "Don't worry, Ang. The kids mostly got pillows and sleeping bags. Sling your pack over your shoulder. Then you'll see what you should really be worrying about."

Oof. He's not joking, but he assures me we'll lighten up fast as we start eating the load.

Katie walks so slowly on the initial road that the forty-seven kilometers seems an impossible goal. She weaves one way and then the other, lazily swinging her limbs, stopping to look at every fallen leaf.

She stops to retie her shoes and then pulls at her shoulder straps. "It's kinda digging in." She squints up at Marty under her ball cap. He pulls off his own pack and leans over her to readjust hers. I imagine us in two weeks: still trekking up this paved road to the trailhead.

"Ang, we're on holidays." Marty doesn't say *relax*. I hate being told to relax. But I get the message. I'm not always good at holidays.

"Okay! Let's count wildlife," I say to distract myself. I take a deep breath and look around, point at the telephone wire over the forest. "One fat robin."

"Whoa!" Ollie separates the grass in the ditch with his foot. "Look! What's that?"

"Dog poo? No wait! A dog-poo colored slug." I pet its long back with my forefinger. Lift it up, twirl its slimy body into my palm to show Katie. "It's camouflaged," I say. "Clever! One fat robin, one slug disguised as dog poo."

"Hey! Hummingbird." Katie moves forward again, with a little more momentum, while Marty readjusts his own pack. A tiny hummingbird buzzes right by Katie's head, and she erupts in giggles. Suddenly, I'm walking through a Disney movie. There's magic everywhere.

"Did you know that chickens are more closely related to dinosaurs than they are to other birds?" Katie lags a bit behind her brother, but her voice is filled with energy and sunlight. Before I have a chance to answer her (*I'm not sure: did I know that?*), she poses another question. "Did you know that hamburgers are named hamburgers because they come from Hamburg?" I think I did know that one, but I don't get out my response before she's off again. Delight at this rare chatter from Katie sends a pleasant buzz through my body. "Did you know that in the morning crocodiles sit toward the sun and open their mouths so that the sun will warm them from the inside?"

"Wait — what?" Marty has broken into a jog to catch us. "Now you're just making stuff up!"

"I'm not. It's true," Katie says, smug. "I did research."

"Did you know that Katie has a *Did You Know* book?" Ollie laughs and Katie joins him, making me hopeful for brother-sister harmony on this vacation.

"Just feel that Day One Magic!" I smile at Marty, grabbing his hand and swinging his arm as we stride up the long hill. On the drive from Fernie, we'd listened to a podcast, *The 3-Day Effect*, about the therapeutic effects of nature with the main premise that campers have to get out in the wild for at least three days to feel the full restorative effects. Three days off phones, three days away from traffic, three days not thinking about work and society.

"It's day *three* magic," Marty corrects me. "Not day one. Stop being an overachiever, Ang. This week we're not racing. We'll get to day three magic when we get there."

"Week week week week," Katie natters happily as she walks. I can't stop smiling. "Week week week week. If you say it enough, it doesn't sound like a word. Week week week week. Try it."

"Week week week," I say. "I feel that way about other words. Like triple. It doesn't seem like a word. Try it: triple triple triple. Or maybe it only seems spelled wrong. It should have two p's — wait . . . What week do you mean? Week as in seven days or weak as in opposite of strong?"

"Seven days."

"Try it with the other weak."

"Weak weak weak weak weak. Same. It doesn't sound like a word, but its spelling makes more sense." Katie makes this declaration with such confident authority, as if it too is a product of her extensive "research."

I notice a pleasant hum radiating from my chest. I evaluate the sensation for a few moments before I recognize it: happiness. Walking this road in the company of my children and my husband, the sun already warm on my skin, the air tasting of ocean, I am happy. We've got a whole week of this: a whole seven days of nothing (no meetings, no practices, no electronics, no school, no social media bullies, nowhere to be, nobody to detract our attention from each other). We can have our meandering, silly conversations at the pace of our meandering walk. We wander, our thoughts wander, our talk wanders. Katie's bubbly chatter infects me, fills me with lightness. By the time we reach the trailhead, our wildlife count includes one fat robin, one tiny hummingbird, and three fat slugs — one black slug, one leopard slug, one dog-poo slug. Each slug spawns a half a dozen ridiculous "why did the slug cross the road" jokes, Marty and Ollie and Katie trying to outdo each other on the scale of absurdity. "Crazy nuts, all of you," I say, maybe only because I'm not as quick-witted as them and can't invent my own slug jokes.

"Yes, but we're your crazy nuts." Marty slings his arm across my shoulders as we walk, and I think he might be just as happy as I am.

Shortly after we transition from paved road to dirt trail, a park ranger pulls up to make sure we've filled in the paperwork and paid our fee with the appropriate envelope in the slot at the trailhead. "There's a mama and two cubs," he tells us. "You'll probably run into them on your second day."

"Mama and cub . . . bears?" Marty leans into the park ranger's truck, and I wonder if I've ever heard my husband ask a dumber question. Maybe Marty likes adopting the clueless tourist role, a welcome change from the responsibility of answering environmental questions every day at work. "Grizzlies?"

"No, we don't have grizzlies on the island. Or actually, we had one last year." The ranger puts his truck into park and turns it off. He seems happy for the company. "The guy kept calling the conservation officer: 'Got a grizzly!' And the officer kept saying, 'Nope, we don't get grizzlies on the island,' so then buddy gets charged by the bear a few times. The third time — it was on First Nations land — buddy pulls out his rifle and shoots the bear, point-blank. Then he calls the conservation officer: 'Come get your grizzly.' So there you go. Turns out we do get grizzlies. Got one again this year."

"They swim all the way over?"

Again I make a face at Marty. How else would the bears get here? Hitchhike? Of course they swim. I try to meet the kids' eyes to share the joke, but they're hurrying ahead, keen to get to the beach.

"Oh yeah — bears are good swimmers. Big and fat. They just float, you know. So the grizzly swims over, eats some food, but then he realizes there's no girls here. And, well you know guys. He hightails it right back to find a girl."

Marty puts his hand on my waist. "If we were grizzlies, I'd swim over to find you."

"Mom. Dad."

"Gross."

It turns out Ollie and Katie are still within hearing range. The ranger starts up his truck and smiles as he slides into drive. "Enjoy your time."

"We will."

Marty and I round the corner to the beach after the kids. Ollie captures my attention as much as the expansive, awe-inspiring view. He stands on the rocky shore, staring out into the ocean, his eyes locked on the point where water meets sky. I could look at his face all day. He's so completely lost in his admiration of landscape, tall and strong, his moppy hair blowing in the sea breeze, his hands tucked under the straps of his big pack, his eyes intense.

"Sorry," he finally says, when he realizes Marty and I are behind him, watching. "It's just . . . amazing." His voice sounds older, more mature, reverent, and I feel tears spring to my eyes. I suppose Ollie apologizes for having lost awareness of us, so completely captured by the natural world. But as soon as he says it, we're gone to him again, his attention returned to the waves. I remember a Buddhist friend explaining happy tears. He said that in those moments where we truly realize the beauty of life, we also realize our own fleeting role. We have both a hold of life's true wonder and an understanding that we must let go. *I am so lucky to have this; I will lose this.*

Originally trained as a Medievalist, I can never help thinking of word origins. The word amazing — which Ollie chose at first sight of Botanical Beach — comes from the Old English *amasian*: to confuse, surprise. That's what the mountains — so very different from the prairie landscape of my childhood — do for me. The shock of extreme difference catapults me into a state of awe. For all of my "Look at the mountains! Look at the mountains!" I know that the alpine landscape does not inspire the same reverent awe in my children. They're used to mountains. But the ocean. The ocean has confused and surprised my son into a state of speechless, immersive wonder.

I watch Ollie for several minutes before looking for Katie. The mix of wind and waves crashing on rocks makes it effortful to speak, and Marty and I don't try, though I see him mutter "wow" under his breath as he moves to follow Ollie along the shoreline. I spot Katie down the beach a bit, tucked over a tide pool, her face down close to the water. I remember Gyllie telling me about the "rich" tide pools on this beach, each full of life. I sit on the sand near Katie and observe her making sense of this underwater world. She has tucked herself so small, a tiny ball in this world of big — big ocean, big waves, big wind, big rocks.

When Marty and Ollie join us, Marty raises his voice above the waves. "We call this Botanical Beach, but the original name, the Indigenous one, means 'Big Wave Beach.'"

"It's like we learned at school," Katie looks up from the pool, but stays on her hands and knees. "About Frank Slide and Turtle

Mountain. The Indigenous people called that place 'the mountain that moves.' They wouldn't live there."

"And then white men built a town in the shadow of the Mountain that Moves, and now that whole town is under boulders as big as houses." I recount the story I've heard so often. "Anna says her ancestors called that mountain Shaky Mountain, and then she always says, 'God, you white folks are stupid. C'mon: *Shaky Mountain*, people!'"

Ollie and Katie laugh, both fans of Anna's big boisterous personality and her in-your-face pronouncements, always delivered with a disarming smile. "Well it is kind of stupid," Ollie says. "Katie's right. The thing with Turtle Mountain really being called Shaky Mountain is just like this place. A beach with big waves — why not call it Big Wave Beach? Why would anyone change that?"

"Anna would say, 'Okay, people, don't build your house on big wave beach. You wouldn't think we'd have to tell you that but —'"

I suspect Katie's laugh comes from the same place as my tears, a release of the surplus of emotion created by this gorgeous world. Laughter or tears: both a physical response to our confusion and surprise — our amazement — that such wonder exists, right here, always.

"So. Kids." Marty slips into instructional mode. Shifting from "Dad on holidays" to "environmental scientist delivering a lecture in his field of expertise," he gathers us into a tight circle. "There're rules. Don't step on lichen. Anything living. Watch where your foot falls. If you step on it, you kill it."

Ollie and Katie nod, serious, and Marty draws a finger around the tide pool Katie had been gazing into, a small deep well with lichen and shells and little fish. "We'll see so many of these, all filled with life. If you've got sunscreen on your hands, or anything at all, do not put them in the tide pools." Marty waves his palms above the water as if washing them but does not dip them below the surface. "Any substance you put on your hands is likely toxic to delicate life."

Again, Ollie and Katie's faces stay solemn and both nod at Marty. I'm relieved to see him break into a smile and lose the professional demeanor. "And just one more rule. Can you guess it?"

"Um . . . have fun, try hard?" Katie recites our family motto, a hint of smile peeking out from under the solemnity.

"Nope. We're on holidays. Forget the trying hard. Just have fun!"

On the trail, Ollie and Katie run ahead of us, their energy seemingly infinite. Katie no longer weaves or lazily swings her long legs. She speeds around corners, under her awkward pack, keeping up with her big brother, leaping easily over old-growth roots that would trip me.

He points to her zipping up a rocky slope and sliding out of view. "Maybe you're right," I say. "I don't have to worry about them keeping up with us. Other way around even."

Beside me Marty takes leisurely strides, pausing to look at the ocean through a break in the trees. He tilts his face up to the sun's heat and takes a deep breath, filling his lungs with the sea breeze. I can see the stress fall away. He looks younger. "I feel better already," he says.

"Me too." I weave my fingers through his. "See. Day One Magic."

By the middle of our first day hiking, the kids have given themselves trail names. Red Cedar for Katie, Rogue Wave for Ollie.

When Marty slips up and calls Katie by her name, she corrects him in her best James Bond impersonation. "Dad, the name is Cedar. *Red Cedar.*"

"Rogue Wave, wait up! Red Cedar, make noise for the bears!" They fly ahead and out of sight, then come racing back, looping around us, long enough to say hi before jetting ahead again, smiles on their faces. Like puppies, they cover two or three times our distance. I wonder if Katie and Ollie will also collapse at the end as Blue would, their tongues stretched out on the ground, happily panting.

"You know who would really love this?" Ollie asks when we stop for an afternoon snack in the trailside shade.

I do know who Ollie means, but I say nothing. I feel our group's temperature dip.

"Blue," he says. "Blue would have loved this."

Back in January, we heard Blue bark at the front door. "This is getting to be a bad habit," I said but rose to let him out.

Blue's friends from down the street — a pug brother-and-sister duo named Diesel and Stitch — often played out front in the quiet cul-de-sac. Stitch would regularly arrive at our door, flat nose pressed wet against the glass, pink collar distinguishing her from her brother.

"Blue, your girlfriend is here!"

We should have shooed all three dogs through the house and into the safe, fenced backyard. But once Blue had a taste of freedom out the front way, he scratched and whined at the door with nerve-rattling persistence. He never went far. He always came home as soon as I called him.

That night, less than ten minutes had passed when I heard a yelping. I jumped to the front door. The cry sounded like Blue but also not like Blue. Higher. More urgent. My eyes found him on the landing below the three steps to our entrance, his black body a shadow. When I opened the door, he tried to stand to meet me, but all four legs slid out from under him. *"He's stuck on the ice,"* I thought. But it was more than the ice. Blue tried so hard to get up, his legs skittering on the shiny ground behind him. I thought: "It's his knees. Oh no! His post-surgery patellas. They're out of joint again." The diagnosis and prognosis ran through my mind: another surgery, thousands of dollars, months of rehab. I resigned myself to the inconvenience and the cost as if, before I bent over to pick Blue up, I'd already struck a deal with nature — *Listen, I'll take the bad knees, please let it be the knees.*

I knew as soon as I touched him. It was not his knees.

By then Marty and Ollie and Katie all stood behind me. I could barely breathe. "He's choking," I said. "Blue!" He sunk into my arms. "Blue! Please!" My fingers went to his jaw. Something was so wrong. His swollen tongue filled his tiny mouth. I didn't know what to do. I pushed the fat slab of tongue down, trying to create space for him to get air.

"Get that out of his mouth! Scoop his mouth!" Marty snapped the commands with atypical urgency.

I can't take it out, Marty. That's his tongue.

I heard the kids saying Blue's name over and over.

"He's dying," I said.

"He's not dying." Marty sounded stern, cross. *Why do you have to be so melodramatic?* That's what I heard. *Why would you say that in front of the kids? You're not helping.*

Before I even got Blue to the living room, Marty had his

sister, the family's only vet, on the phone. "His tongue? Purple. No grey. Blue. Blue-ish grey." Marty kept his voice serious but not loud or urgent. He wore the artificial calm he reserved for crises.

"Don't die! Don't Die! Blue, don't die!" Ollie yelled the words like a command. *Sit, speak, don't die.* A mournful wail came from Katie. I closed my eyes in apology. Why did I say it?

"He's going to be okay," I lied. "Everything's going to be okay."

"Put him down." Marty pointed to the area rug in the living room and dialed a new number (animal crisis line, he mouthed). *Go,* I tried to say to the kids, *go upstairs now.* But they didn't go. I stuck my fingers down Blue's throat trying to dislodge some imagined object, but I found nothing. As I lowered Blue's warm body to the ground, one big drop of blood fell from his mouth, splattered on the floor. Katie held both hands over her face and screamed "No no no no no no! Blue!"

"Grey," Marty said into the phone. "His tongue is grey. His eyes are glassy. No, no blinking." He pushed me aside long enough to hold his hand to Blue's chest. "No. Nothing."

I found the spot that must house Blue's tiny heart. I pressed pressed pressed, lowered my mouth toward his snout. I put my fingers back to his little furry chest, thinking of the baby mannequins of my teenage lifeguarding courses. I pushed those two fingers firm into the flesh where I imagine his heart to be. "Blue," I whispered. "*Please.* Blue."

"Ang."

Don't be soft. Be mad. Be angry at me for saying Blue was dying. I should never have said that. Blue's not dying.

Marty's hand fell heavy to my shoulder. His phone sat on the coffee table, the screen dark. "Ang."

"He's dead," I said. "I know it. He's dead." I didn't lift my hands from Blue's thick fur to dry my soaked face.

"Let me take him."

"No no no no no no no." The kids, who rarely reacted the same, now howled in unison. I didn't move my lips but the word filled me: *no no no no no no no no.* I buried my nose in Blue's rich mane, cried into his fur.

By our second lunch on Juan de Fuca Trail, we have only crossed paths with seven people. We always smile our way toward oncoming hikers, our friendliness mirrored in their own expressions.

"It's beautiful, isn't it?!"

"Yes, so beautiful!"

We encounter no animosity. Already, I barely believe in the hostility and conflict that have become so common in my day-to-day online life, the kind of meanness that has spilled over into my offline communities.

"People are so nice," I say to Marty. "Everyone's so happy. I forgot people can be so nice. I remember now: I used to like people. What a couple of years —"

"Stop! Remember the day-three-magic podcast!"

"What?"

"Remember the monitors? Even *thinking* about stress registered as stress in the body."

He's right. The campers in *The 3-Day Effect* wore devices to measure stress as indicated by various bodily factors. Each participant could link spikes in stress to moments in which they let their thoughts draw back to troubles at home. "We're not going to think about any of it," Marty insists. "Not about Facebook fights or

Twitter squabbles or online bullies. We're not going to think about credit card bills or house repairs or staff shortages or selenium in the river or —"

"Stop! I bet your stress is already spiking off the chart." Dealing with selenium in the local river is one of Marty's most taxing work challenges.

"Not thinking about it."

"Okay. Deal. I will think only about trees."

Ollie voices his enthusiasm as we move through the days: *Wow! Look at that!* But Katie, despite her day-one giddiness, stays mostly quiet. She makes herself small in the face of nature, squeezing into hollow tree trunks, crouching over tide pools. Thanks to many winter days searching for fairies in the forest with her dad, Katie believes in the magic of nature. "She's so beautiful," I say to Marty. "I lied to Gyllie, you know? I told her we had experience with overnight backpacking trips with kids." We'd done multiday canoe trips with camping, and single-day hiking trips with no camping. I figured this trip just combined both. "I didn't want her to think me rash. And I knew Katie could do it. Even if she couldn't, then we turn back. No big deal. Right?"

"Katie! I mean, Red Cedar! Look!" Marty has found a big leaf in the middle of the trail with a face punched out, two holes for eyes and a curving line for a mouth. "It's Groot!"

Katie laughs, delighted, and points to a giant tree down the path. "That looks like Groot too!"

Looking for Groots slows her a bit, forces her to keep pace with Marty and me. We soon realize that hikers have left leaves with faces all along the trail. "It must be fairies," Marty says. Even Ollie, not a fairy believer, grows animated when we arrive at a clearing and find a whole family of leaf-people or round a corner to a herd of particularly scary leaf-faces or look up to the surprise of a leaf-person hanging from a branch. I prefer the children hiking alongside us like this, not only because the point of the trip is to spend time together, but also because I worry about their safety when they wander too far ahead. I know Sinead, who cofounded the outdoor school in Fernie, encourages risky play and argues we must allow children to set their own boundaries, within reason, and thereby learn the consequences of extending too far. But I also think about Peter Wohlleben's *The Hidden Life of Trees*. Wohlleben explains the social interaction of trees, showing them to be interconnected beings, influenced by their own social and familial connections. He explains that the big, parental trees shade the small ones, blocking infant trees from the sun so they don't grow up too fast. Slowing the growth of baby trees ensures they don't sprout into semi-adulthood before they have the strength and nutrients necessary to thrive. I'm happy to keep these two saplings of mine in our shade for a good while longer.

I favor the midway approach of Ellen Beate Hansen Sandseter, a professor of early childhood education in Norway. She advocates for *controlled* risk. We can eliminate the perils children do not yet have the ability to handle while also letting them navigate the risks they can. To determine which is which, parents need to ask themselves three questions: Will the children be able to anticipate the danger? Is it a danger that could cause life-threatening harm? Is it a risk that could lead to a positive learning experience?

In *Free-Range Kids: How to Raise Safe, Self-Reliant Children (without Going Nuts with Worry)*, Lenore Skenazy suggests introducing each new activity in steps, talking through the potential hazards to make kids aware of the danger, and then easing away from parental supervision as the children demonstrate understanding. By gradually increasing their exposure to controlled risk, we focus on preparedness rather than protection. Skenazy's own experience focuses on big city risks: don't stand too close to the tracks, don't talk to strangers, learn how to read a map, know who to ask for help. Her strategy, though, easily translates to the wild: be aware of your surroundings; make lots of noise so bears know you're coming; if you see an animal, assume a non-threatening posture and back slowly away. By accompanying children, alerting them to the risks, and demonstrating smart behavior, we can gradually let them out of parental shelter by increments, as they — and their parents — feel ready.

Marty handled all the details of Blue's death.

Marty moved Blue's cooling body to the garage, wrapped him in a camping blanket, and maneuvered him into the kennel. He arranged for the autopsy and the cremation, canceled the pet insurance, and picked up the urn of ashes.

"I should do some of these unpleasant tasks," I said.

"Let me do it," Marty requested. "I didn't do anything that night. As soon as things went wrong, I got on the stupid phone. I stepped away. Let me at least take care of you guys now."

"No, Marty! You did exactly what you needed to do. If you hadn't had the calmness of mind to get on the phone with experts, we never would've known if we did all we could for Blue."

In the coming weeks, we would all find fault with ourselves. But that night, after Marty stored Blue's body in the garage, we did not talk about blame. Ollie pressed his palms hard into his face, drying his tears. "I need some air," he declared like a middle-aged man wiped out after a bad day at work. Moved by his sudden decisiveness, we all robotically piled on our winter layers and followed Ollie out into the dark. To those looking onto the snowy street, unable to see Katie's swollen, red-rimmed eyes, we must have painted a sweet picture, our whole family on a late-night stroll to enjoy the quiet falling flakes.

Ollie and Katie led, while Marty and I followed behind like baby ducklings. Anyone seeing us trudging down the street would attribute the hunch of our shoulders and the drop of our heads to the cold weather. None of us spoke.

After fifteen minutes, Ollie stopped. "Okay," he said. "I'm done. I'm going back." Still silent, the three of us turned and followed him home.

In the lit-up house, I saw that Katie's face had turned a scary white, and her thin body still shook with sobs, but Ollie's face was dry. "Well," he said. "There's nothing we can do. I think we should put this whole night out of our minds. Being sad doesn't help. Blue would have wanted us to move on and be happy." Numb, I turned to Marty, wanting to share a smile about our strange twelve-year-old son talking like a grown-up grief counselor. But I couldn't make my face move.

Katie hiccupped through her final sobs, wiped her nose, and then finally spoke, as if angry: "We are *never* getting another dog."

The autopsy results arrived a week later. A vehicle hit Blue. The impact ruptured his diaphragm. Material from his stomach filled his lungs. After the collision, he would not have been able to breathe at all. The accident must have happened right in front of our house. He made it home on his final breath.

"Getting home was Blue's last heroic act," Ollie said with a solemn expression. "He did it for you."

"Let's make a pact," I said to Marty months later, in the early spring. "If either one of us starts getting really weird in old age, we'll say so. We'll stop each other from developing too many eccentricities."

"Ang. You run with a dog's ashes in your pocket. I think that ship might have sailed." But he said it with a smile. He knew by then that I needed the trails: my mental health and happiness depended on the woods, and my family's well-being depended on my mental health and happiness. If I needed a dog's ashes to get me back out there, then I should run with the dog's ashes.

The new sleep system works exactly as Marty promised. We sleep double, snuggled together in the middle of the tent with a child on each side. Ollie pushes far enough into the tent wall that he can pretend he's sleeping alone, while I often wake with Katie curled warm into my side. We crawl into our sleeping bags so full-body exhausted that even the hard ground welcomes us. But we never fall straight asleep. The group dynamic brings Sleepover Party Katie to life, and she fills the space with her silly chatter. Each time we've all nearly sunk into full slumber, her voice breaks the silence.

"Dad?"

"Katie!" Ollie is in less of a party mood. "Enough. Go to sleep."

"Yes, sweetie?" Marty asks, overruling Ollie's order.

"Is caramel popcorn a sweet snack or a savory snack?"

"Katie! Seriously. Stop!" Suddenly, Ollie is the one telling Katie not to talk so much? Personalities do contain multitudes.

"That's a fantastic question, Katie. I think you've lit upon one of the age-old mysteries of the universe. Salty yet sweet. Caramel popcorn defies categorization."

I don't say anything, just listen. These silly conversations delight me as much in the dark as they did on our morning walk to the trailhead. We have nothing serious to talk about and no reason to go to sleep early. At home, Marty, never a good sleeper, would be stressed about his early morning departure for work. He'd be stomping around, filling his lunchbox and grumping that it'd gotten too late, the kids should be asleep, and he still had chores to do. He'd be counting the hours until five a.m., when he had to get up. In our tent, I put my arm around his chest, tuck myself into his warmth, and listen to him and Katie classify candy apples, pickled beets, gummy worms, and sweet bread.

We're halfway into the hike and nothing has happened. No bear encounters. No injuries. No getting lost. In fact, what's "not happening" has become a focus of our days. The kids loved Monday morning, day three, when they realized they would normally be in school. They checked their watches throughout the day: math not happening, science not happening, recess not happening, swim club not happening. They delighted in the magic of stepping out of the day-to-day script and replacing it with nothing, or with the deliberate lack of structure of walking and forest and ocean.

Nothing happening is the very definition of a successful wilderness trip, whereas something happening is the essential requirement of a successful story. This far into my iPhone detox, I recognize my constant pull to the phone as a desire for something always to be happening. In any moment of lull in regular life, I reach for the phone. But maybe some kind of day three magic really has soaked in, because I do not miss my phone one bit.

"Dad's taking us out for dinner! C'mon, kids!" I step down onto the rocky shore. The tide is out and I've never seen so many mussels in my life. Shellfish glued to the rocks, everywhere. Hundreds of them. "It's a seafood restaurant!"

Really, we will crouch down on a hard, sharp cliff and eat crunchy dehydrated something-or-other (Italian pasta, Thai curry, Korean bibimbap — it all tastes the same — and no matter how long we let it soak in boiled water, it still has little floaty cardboard bits). Still, we have read enough about tourists poisoned by shellfish on this coast to avoid the mouth-watering temptation to steam up some mussels. Recreational harvesting is now illegal. Commercial harvesters test for toxins.

Marty kneels over his ultralight camping stove, sheltering it from the wind until the flame connects. Once he's got the water on to boil, he sets some rocks up as a buffer and moves to sit next to me, resting his arm across my shoulders. We're both puffed up in our down jackets, and I smile at the teddy-bear quality of the hug, pulling him closer into my feathery self. "Fine dining," he says. "Do I know how to show a girl a good time or what?"

"Best restaurant I've ever been to." I kiss his cheek, rough with five days' growth.

A sign pounded into the rocks warns *Rogue Waves!* Massive rolls of white foam crash around us. Katie and Ollie have climbed onto a huge black rock and sit side by side, looking onto the expanse of sea. If I'd brought my phone, I'd get a picture of them there together, the image of brother-sister happiness. Marty and I didn't pack any alcohol on the trip, but I feel pleasantly intoxicated, filled with downy warmth.

"Don't they ever get tired?" I weave my fingers into Marty's, watching Katie jump from the big rock and run to the next, stretching her thin arms high to get a good hold, straining to pull herself up. "Hey! Red Cedar! Rogue Wave! Careful!"

"They're having fun."

"These rocks are so sharp, though." I'm pretty comfortable, and not too alarmed, but my skin hurts watching Katie's gangly race across the jagged ground. I feel the possibility of her tripping with every step. I yell, unable to resist my own job description. Mother: 1) worry; 2) nag. "You two! Don't fall yourselves to death!"

"They're fine."

"Sure, that's what you say. Until a rogue wave sweeps Ollie out to sea and his nickname proves prescient."

"Ang." Marty cocks his head. *Really?* That's what this gesture means. I know it well. "If that happens, it was meant to be. If someone's going to go, I don't know a cooler way than a rogue wave."

Ollie and Katie both have a healthy flush to their cheeks. Ollie worries me by venturing out toward the edge, too close to the colossal waves, Katie by always testing her climbing abilities, higher and higher. As soon as she summits one boulder, she leaps off and races to a bigger one. "Don't they ever simply walk anywhere?"

"You haven't been writing," Marty says, pouring boiling water into our packet of dinner. He looks healthy too, his face bronzed by the week outdoors. I like the silver highlights in his scruff. I reach out and stroke the back of my hand against his cheek. We talked about writing before we left, my pens and journals an issue in our battle against the scale, our goal of going extra light.

"No writing. Lots of thinking." In the spring, unsure what direction this book would take, I'd joked that I'd pen a Murakami-inspired *What I Talk about When I Talk about Dragging My Whining Kids down the Juan de Fuca Trail in the Pouring Rain*. Our adventure has gone so much more smoothly than it might have.

"What're you thinking about?"

"Mmm. How writing pulls me out of an experience? Whenever a writer tells me about anything significant happening in their life, my first question is always, *Are you going to write about it?* As if life is, above all else, material for a book. I catch myself treating my own life like that, *our lives*, always standing a little bit outside of what's going on and thinking how I can shape it into a story."

"Right. Okay. But you already committed to a hiking book, didn't you?"

"Yeah. And I'll write it. But I wonder if the act of looking actually changes something, like I can't be in the moment enjoying you and Katie and Ollie because I'm standing outside of that moment as a writer observing. I do want to be in this moment, here. Here is good." I lift our entwined hands and kiss the back of his. "Really good."

"Fifteen minutes until dinner, you guys!" The wind seems to blow Marty's announcement right back to us, but Ollie and Katie look our way and nod.

"A critic of *Home Ice* said the book wasn't really about hockey, and I should've called it *Angie Figures out Life*. My first response was, *Awesome! Bookish middle-aged woman figures out life*. That's always my goal, in writing and reading. To reach toward and artic-ulate meaning, to deepen my understanding of life . . . and self."

I blush a little. Marty's more of a doer than a reader or writer, and I rarely talk this way to him. "But in middle age, I'm deciding maybe I don't always have to have the pen in my hand. Maybe I can enjoy the experience for the experience, and still maybe hold onto enough of that life that I can do the figuring out part, the writing part, later."

"What part of this trip will you hold onto, do you think?"

"I keep coming back to the idea of being a tourist, how it changes things. This morning on the beach when we saw that vertical garden, Scarlet Paintbrush growing right out of the rock wall, the kids . . . they really *looked*, you know? Stopped hard in their tracks and stared. We have that kind of beauty at home, but we don't take the time to look like that. As tourists, our sole purpose is *to look*. Even now," I point out to Ollie and Katie. "The joy they're taking in these rocks. We have rocks at home."

Marty doesn't respond, and I don't elaborate. Too often I need to verbalize every thought that comes into my mind. As I get used to "nothing happening," I don't feel that same pull. I lean against the rock, huddled under my husband's warm arm, and we watch our children play.

My most recent experience of being an international tourist came this past winter. LASALLE College of the Arts in Singapore invited me to speak and lead some workshops for graduate students. The host suggested I take a side trip while on that side of the world: "The best thing about Singapore is how many cool places you can get to from here. Cheap. Pick one. I'll add four days on your ticket." I didn't know if I could hack four days traveling solo in a big city. But I knew I would be perfectly happy wandering alone exploring temples. I picked Cambodia. I watched the sun rise over Angkor Wat. I meandered through Cambodian jungle, climbing on ruins. I ate lunches so fresh and flavorful that I would travel all the way around the world again if only for another bowl of soup.

I started to feel less euphoric about my role as tourist when a middle-aged woman offered to paddle me out to look at a floating village. She held out a sun umbrella, indicating that I could protect myself with shade while she did all the work in the deadly heat so I could get a close-up look at how very little these people had.

I wondered what we would call this. Poverty tourism?

I didn't want to go. I already felt uncomfortable, staring at the homes from a distance. Did these people want me floating by their private homes, gawking? No, I couldn't imagine that they did. But a male guide, the one with the best English, pushed me. "She'll take you. She wants to. Yes. This money goes for this village. It's important. They need your money." He pointed out which of my bills would be sufficient, and I passed them to him, then I clumsily climbed into the back of the long narrow boat floating on brown water. The smiling woman in the bow thrust her umbrella toward me. I tried to hold it at an angle to shade both of us as she paddled through the muddy water under the violent midday sun.

People here lived with so little. Home was a piece of plywood on top of some floating tires, maybe another piece of plywood over top for shade. A few of these dwellings had flowers out front or an extra raft attached alongside, creating room for a couple of penned-in chickens or a small garden. Kids in their underwear jumped into the brown water, splashing and laughing. Dozens of tourist boats circled them. We passed a floating school, two floating churches, a floating store, a floating gas station. I wanted the whole thing to be over — not because I felt uncomfortable seeing the poverty, but because I felt uncomfortable with these Cambodian people seeing me see it. They weren't creatures in a zoo, there for my amusement after I'd paid admission. If this smiling woman and I spoke the same language, I would have given her another fifty dollars right there to paddle me out.

After my boat tour, instead of jumping on the bus, I bought two cans of cold beer, sought out the guide with the strong English, and found us a spot in the shade.

I asked him straight out: "Is tourism good for you? Has it changed anything for the better in any way? For you? For your family?"

"No." He had been smiley when he encouraged me onto the boat, but now his face grew grim. He dropped the tour-guide facade. "Prices of everything have gone up. All these people come, and we see what we can't have. I watch people in restaurants. I'd like to try that food. But we can never try the food. If I go ask them for a taste, even of the food they don't eat, the owner will chase me out. He will throw the food in the garbage, not give it to me. I'd like to tell those tourists: take the extra food in a bag. Give it to the poor people in the street. We'd like to try that food. I could take some home for my kids."

I asked how old his kids were, and he told me he had a twelve-year-old boy and a ten-year-old girl. The same as Ollie and Katie. I held the cool beer up to my cheek and watched a group of men try to convince tourists to paddle out to the floating village. A cage at our feet housed a crocodile. It looked thirsty.

"My wife died two years ago, from bad water. She was twenty-three. Now I raise the two kids myself. Because of tourism, they see every day what they can't have." He gestured to me, everything about me an example of what he and his family did not have. "My son, he's old enough to know how hard I work so he asks for nothing. He pretends to be okay with what we have. My daughter, she doesn't understand. Too young. She always asks for what she sees. Now she wants a backpack. I tell her no, the plastic bag works better, so you don't get your books wet. You use the plastic bags. Maybe one day I can afford for her a backpack."

I thought of my house in Fernie, full of unused backpacks. "I wondered if maybe Cambodia had a two-tier pricing system," I said. "Like one price for tourists and one for locals."

"No." He bit his bottom lip as he shook his head. "At first yes, but then no. If a businessman can get two dollars for a Coke instead of fifty cents, or fifteen dollars for dinner instead of two dollars, why would he give his product away for less? Same with everything: always costs more."

"What about this tourism?" I gestured at the boats. "You told me my money went to villagers? That helps?"

He didn't speak for a while and then he met my eyes in a way that made me flinch. "What," he asked, "is the one nice thing about this life, one that you can see?"

I thought for a moment. "The kids jumping off their front porches. Playing in the water." Like living in the middle of a swimming pool.

"Yes, it used to be. Now the boats come by. Always the boats. The big ones make waves and drive so close to the houses, so everyone can get their pictures of their holiday. This year already, in the wake of those boats, three children have drowned."

The man thanked me for the beer and for my tourist dollars. He smiled at me. But I rode the bus back to my nine-dollar-a-night hotel heavy with guilt.

"Whoa! Look at that tree!" Katie has come to a standstill midtrail and points at the forest.

"What tree?" Ollie laughs. "There's lots of trees."

But I see the one she means: a true giant.

"Holy," Marty says. "A wolf tree in an old-growth forest. I bet that's a thousand years old."

"Before the Norman Conquest," Ollie comments and gives me a sidelong glance, knowing I'll be impressed by his historical knowledge and his quick math. He hasn't given his attention over to the tree.

"Look." Marty grabs Katie by the hand and pulls her into the forest, touches the massive trunk. "One of its branches alone is as big as an entire old-growth tree." I love this Marty so very much, there with his hand on the tree's trunk, his eyes on its enormous branches. "There are old-growth trees growing out of that old-growth tree."

"That's incredible!" Now Ollie noisily trudges through the ground cover toward them, his head tilted way back to take in the tree's canopy. "Fhaaaa." He lets out a noise of inarticulate awe.

We decide to have lunch at the tree's base and scrape together our last bits of food: four packets of miso soup, some handfuls of trail mix, a power bar for each of us. We're slow to leave the forest and continue to move at a slug's pace through the afternoon, knowing we've reached our final day, reluctant to emerge from the woods.

We must be within a kilometer of the trail's conclusion when we meet a park ranger. "Run into any bears?" he asks.

"Not one," Marty says, as if disappointed. "Not even much scat."

"Yeah, the bears mostly stay down at the beach. Basically bears are lazy. They've got an all-you-can-eat buffet of mussels down there. Why go anywhere else? They lounge at the beach, gorge themselves on easy-to-get seafood, and then poo on the service roads."

"Not the worst life." Marty laughs before waving farewell to the ranger and following Ollie and Katie down to the water.

Marty finds a big log to lean against and stretches his legs out in the pebbles. The sun occasionally peeks out from the clouds, but the air's too cool for swimming. Ollie and Katie both run right to the water, still wearing their boots. Since it's the last day, I let them. Marty digs into his pack, shuffles around, finally emerging with a dirty strip of beef jerky. "Last piece!" He breaks it in half and hands a portion to me.

"Aw. You do love me," I say, tearing at the chunk of hard meat with my back teeth. "I'm fucking filthy. You know what's gonna be good? A shower. A hot, hot shower."

"I don't want to go," Marty says.

"I think we've gotta go." I put a hand on his shoulder and lower myself onto the pebbly beach next to him. Five nights in a tent has done a number on my back. I am going to love my bed.

"Nope. I'm staying. I'll be a resident of Juan de Fuca Trail. I'll eat the mussels. I'll poo on the service roads."

I say nothing. Katie's up to her knees in the ocean now, boots and all, a decision that has clearly stressed out her big brother. Eventually, Ollie coaxes her out of the water.

Katie has, in the last three days, decided that when she grows up, she's going to the University of Victoria. She's never been to

Victoria, and I imagine she expects it to be exactly like Juan de Fuca Trail.

I point to Katie as she and her brother trudge up the beach. "You look like you're bringing the ocean home in your socks!"

"I'd love to bring this *all* home," Marty sighs.

"Maybe we can bring home some of the mood we found here." I'm thinking aloud, relaxed. "You know how we're tourists here but locals at home. Maybe we can be tourists at home. In the way that we look at everything; we're open to wonder. But also locals in the sense that we want to care for the place and ensure the best of it lasts."

Katie plops down on the rocks and pulls off her boots and wet socks, as if she intends to hike the last kilometer in bare feet.

Ollie looks anxious. "What time are we catching the shuttle? Shouldn't we go?"

At the shuttle stop, we meet a young couple gearing up to begin the trail. They look so clean. "Wow," the fresh-faced woman says. "Your whole family did it! The entire trail?"

Marty and I nod proudly.

"And how old are you?" She points her question at Katie.

Katie holds the stranger's eyes and says in a strong, clear voice "Ten. And my brother is twelve. We had every campground to ourselves except for one. I don't like when there are other people in the campground."

I don't comment on Katie's shyness or lack thereof, consciously resisting that urge to constantly evaluate, but I do wordlessly note the difference one good week can make. "It's true. She does not like sharing a campground. She's so spoiled she doesn't even know she's spoiled," I laugh. "But she did great." I put my arm around Katie's shoulders, help her off with her pack. "They both did. And the hike is gorgeous. You'll see. You're going to enjoy every minute of that trail."

"You really will," Marty agrees. "We had an amazing week."

"Absolutely perfect," I add. "Nothing at all happened."

Five

Fires, Cliffs, Bears, Booze, Drugs, and All the Parental Nightmares

After our Juan de Fuca trip, rain dominates the spring, chasing us off the trails. I've grown used to summer playing hard to get in the mountains. One wet July, years ago when Katie was still a baby, I hauled my miserable self out for a jog, knowing the combination of fresh air and elevated heartrate to be the only cure for my most violent funks. On an uphill, less than a kilometer from my house, I ran into an outdoorsy, mountain-loving woman I'd known for decades. She stood astride her bike, gazing into the sodden woods, her jacket soaked, her pants splattered with mud, her hair dripping. She had a thin, athletic frame, and if I didn't know her to be in her forties, I would think she were a teenager. I readied myself to download my gloom about the horrible, debilitating, ruinous, suicide-inducing wet weather of the past three months. She stopped me with her smile. "Isn't it beautiful?" she said. "So fresh. So green." She took a deep breath. I could see her joy, in the sheen of her eyes, the upturn of her face. "I just love it. I guess that's why we live in a rain forest. We're so lucky."

The perspective shift gave me whiplash. I swallowed my complaints. "Yes," I said, adopting a smile and pretending conviction, "lucky us."

Now, when I'm rain-glum, I try to summon the memory of her bright smile and her enthusiasm for the rain forest. *Lucky us!* I can do it too, once I'm out the door. Some days, though, the initial hurdle over the threshold — and into the wall of grey — is insurmountable.

This year we have another reason, beyond the fresh and the green, to praise the rain. All over town, in place of a regular greeting, people sing:

"At least it's not smoky!"

"This should keep away the season's fires!"

"Rain! Thank god!"

"Maybe, with some luck, we'll get through the whole summer without a campfire ban!"

I'm heartened by their insistent glee in the face of the cold, the wet, the grey, but I also find their gratitude alarming. We have arrived at a point where we must express thanks for every summer month that doesn't bring the threat of fire.

Last summer, at the peak of local wildfires, I realized that Ollie and Katie will probably not remember a non-smoky July, or an August with fire-roasted marshmallows, or a summer news cycle without a tally of nearby evacuations. For them, summer season means fire season. In August 2018, *Harper's Magazine* published a particularly apocalyptic article pointing the finger of wildfire blame to our spreading human population. One of the main

culprits? Houses in the wildland-urban interface. People who want
to live close to nature have built their homes on the outskirts of
town at the forest's edge, not only putting themselves in danger
of natural forest fires but also providing a path for sparks to leap
through to town.

We are exactly those kind of people. Plus, we can't reassure
ourselves with a perky "it'll never happen here" because our little
mountain town *has* burned to the ground. Twice.

So this spring, Marty and I sing along with everyone else:
"Thank goodness for all this rain!"

When the sun rallies in late June, I am keen to get out into the
backcountry, but we decide to stick to low elevation. Higher up,
all the moisture has been snow, pushing hiking season — and my
and Katie's peak-a-week challenge — into July. Instead, for our
Father's Day outing, I plan a small hike for our whole family —
more of a walk really — at the most beautiful place I know, only a
half-hour drive from our house. A couple of decades ago, Marty
and I and our crowd imagined the secluded spot to be our secret,
an enchanted alternate world for aimless twenty-somethings to
sprawl on sun-warmed cliffs high above sea-green water. Beer.
Bikinis. Pot. Music. The occasional shriek as a friend threw herself
into the icy lake below.

Now this gorgeous spot is included in every local guidebook,
with pictures, description, and detailed directions. It even has a
parking lot of sorts, and a well-marked trailhead.

With each step up the rocky slope, Marty clanks, his backpack
full of expired bear spray canisters. Water trickles down the path
and over the black rocks so they glisten in the sun, and I warn the

kids to watch their step. I wonder if my parents could handle this walk. I'd love to show them these lakes, the magic of where we live, but I don't think my father, with his two artificial hips, could manage the combination of steep and slippery, even though it's not far.

Katie and I have veered left onto a shortcut, but we can still see — and hear — Marty and Ollie to our right, just through the trees, both of them breathing hard in their attempt to beat us to the top.

"Dad. I'm just saying. I think this is a bad idea." Ollie has been expressing his negative opinion of Marty's idea ever since we pulled out of the driveway with a truck bed full of bear spray. "Really, really stupid bad."

"Well I think it's a *great* idea," Katie chirps, leaping awkwardly over a stream that will disappear as soon as we hit summer proper. I flinch as she lands on the damp rocks, but she catches her balance to continue racing upward.

Ollie squishes his facial features together, in a parodic imitation of Katie's pronounced cheeks, and sets his voice to a high-pitched squeak, mimicking: "*I think it's a great idea.*" He releases his face to its usual preteen pout and drops his tone. "Suck-up."

"Ollie, stop it."

"Om," I think. "Ommmm."

On the Juan de Fuca Trail, I read Haruki Murakami's *What I Talk about When I Talk about Running*. The book disappointed me at its initial publication in 2007. I'd long felt on the verge of having something profound (but just out of reach) to say about the role of physical activity, its connection to meditative states and to deep, creative thought, as well as something about the ways sport gives meaning and structure to life, the lessons the body-in-motion can teach. I didn't find that out-of-reach "something" in Murakami's pages. But revisiting the book in 2019, twelve years older and recently turned fifty, I saw Murakami's insights differently. This time, I dog-eared the book so badly that I transformed the pages into origami. Now, in proper middle age, I recognize the simple wisdom of Murakami's words. He says we do physical activity for the feeling it gives us in our heart. He says by working to overcome physical pain, we arrive at a quality of being whole. He says he writes about running to try to understand what running means. I see his keyword as *try*: we may strive toward understanding but never reach it. He says that competition comes down to only one question: am I better than I was yesterday? Though, as we age, better can't mean only faster and stronger, or we will eventually fail. Can better mean something else? Less distracted. More connected to the physical world, rather than using it only as a static backdrop to our activity. Calmer in our minds.

But as Katie and Ollie bicker their way up the slick slope to the first lake, I do not feel calm in my mind. I wonder if, in order to reap Murakami's contemplative, restorative benefits of outdoor activity, one must be *alone*. I would like right now to be alone, with the damp forest, the late June sun hot on my skin, the pristine lake luring me upward.

"Well it's dumb. The bear spray is called *expired* for a reason. It's called *bear* spray for a reason. I just don't see why we would —"

"Ollie." Annoyance sharpens Marty's voice. All this rain, and its run-off, has made Marty's day job taxing. When the rain carries the wrong substances down into our river, people bring their complaints and concerns directly to Marty. *Fix it, and fix it now.* Fair requests, both of them. Into the silence that his sharp *Ollie* created, I watch Marty crack his neck severely to the right and then to the left. I know the gesture well: him pushing back against his own stress. *We're here to have fun, dammit, to be happy.* When Marty speaks again, he has managed to rid his voice of its edge. "Check out Super Cliff!"

We've popped up to a view of the first lake, a startling aqua green surrounded by steep rock faces. When ravaged by smoke, as we were earlier this month before we left for Juan de Fuca Trail at the start of June, we believe in climate change, know the end must be near, but here in this crisp air with the inviting clear, clean water, we forget. How can *this* be dying? It's perfect.

We still have to trek around the water to get to the first jumping spot, but I count a couple of dozen sunbathers, music blaring. They sprawl on cliffs high above us, though still far below the crazy ledge Marty calls Super Cliff. I picture him jumping from that spot in his twenties, sixty feet down to the water, falling and falling and still falling.

We've formed into single file on the narrow trail weaving us around the first lake. Marty leads, but Katie skips right on his heels. "Was it fun?! Super Cliff, super fun?!"

I stay at the back of our little group, aiming to rest my mind on the scenery, a view so delicious I want to drink it.

"Yep. Super fun!"

"*Marty,*" I say, my attention slipping from the view. "Really?"

"Well, I did hurt myself a bit one time. Diving. I was going so fast by the time I hit. When I tucked my head to roll underwater, I strained all the muscles in my neck. It hurt for three days. Probably not the best idea."

"Mmm," I say. "Probably not."

We pull to the side of the trail to let a family slip past us on their way down, two teenage boys and a sunburned mom and dad. They greet us lazily, sun-saturated. Katie looks to her feet instead of saying hi. How can a girl so intrigued by the sixty-foot Super Cliff, a girl who was so giddy on the Juan de Fuca Trail, be too scared to say hello to a small group of friendly strangers? Ollie snaps out of his funk long enough to be polite, but once the group passes, he slinks back into his shadow. Out of their hearing range, he sulks: "Do we have to swim?"

"Ollie," I hear my own annoyance now, an echo of Marty. This spring-fed water stays brain-freeze icy all year round, and I would never *make* anyone swim. I could simply say, *No, Ollie, you don't have to swim.* "Go back and sit in the truck for all I care," I snap. "You don't have to do anything."

"Good. If I don't have to do anything, I'm not doing the bear spray."

"Bud. Lighten up." The edge has sliced back in Marty's voice too. "We're *all* doing the bear spray."

"I'll do his bear spray!" Katie grabs the trunk of a tree and swings herself around it, left leg extended, a big grin on her face, like nothing could be more delightful than her brother's miserable mood. She's recently shaved half her head. She wanted a Mohawk but, in light of my objections, settled for a severe undercut. "I don't see the big deal. It grows back. I like to use my hair to express myself."

I hated the thought of shearing her stunning auburn hair but reminded myself: her head, not mine. I have to admit, the asymmetrical style looks cute on her, one side hanging at a sharp angle to her chin beneath her rainbow ball cap. Unique, like her.

"Katie, stop. Don't aggravate Ollie. Let's just enjoy the view. Enjoy the day." *Ommmmm.*

"I'm going to swim. I'm going to do Super Cliff."

"Of course she is. She would. She's that stu—"

"Ollie. Nobody is stupid. Nobody is doing Super Cliff." I take deep, deliberate breaths. "Please. Stop." I had a simple plan for today: family, nature, fun. We have all the right ingredients. And the setting: perfect spring weather in a place of unmatched beauty.

Everyone stays quiet, but the silence doesn't feel comfortable or serene. It's electric with aggravation. I'm the first to talk. "Actually, speaking of Super Cliff. You guys need to learn to be smart. Nature is dangerous. People have died here. Kids drinking and diving. Imagine that — your friend bleeding at the bottom of a cliff, unconscious, you having to hike out to the road to get cell service, waiting for an ambulance to arrive, waiting for first responders to get up that hill with a spinal board, not knowing if your friend — or maybe your sister or brother — would live or die."

"Ang." Marty says the syllable softly, as if to pull me back to myself. This day keeps inching further away from my vision of it, the reality a parody of my intention.

"Well, I'm ten!" There's a giggle in Katie's words. She's the only one of us not infected by the day's dirty mood. "I don't drink beer. Or go cliff diving with my friends. I guess you don't need to worry about me."

We've made our way high on the rocks, looking down at the lake. Local guidebooks describe the water many different ways, ranging from deep blue to aqua to green to clear. Today, emerald fits best, a green so bright it seems artificial, like costume jewelry. I imagine the lake as a color-shifting mood ring, taking the emotional temperature of its surroundings; I decide this green must signify irritated, at the least.

Really, the most common backcountry injuries involve neither drunk stunts (my fear) nor bear attacks (the disaster Marty plans to educate us against today). Dozens of separate studies list less dramatic ways to ruin a hiking adventure: twisted ankles, camp-fire burns, dehydration, bee stings, bad blisters.

I'm being gloomy, lecturing. I search for Scarlet Paintbrush, my favorite wildflower, something beautiful to help me push a reset on the tone of this adventure. But no wildflowers have bloomed yet in the Rockies, the season's growth delayed by the cool spring.

"How's *your* back doing?" Marty rests a hand under my pack, smiles. *We're here to have fun, dammit, to be happy.*

"Okay." I sigh the word, refusing to elaborate.

I do not want to talk about my back. I got an X-ray of my spine the week before, a picture I wish I'd never seen — a map of past accidents and a harrowing prediction of future pain. I knew of each accident already, of course, but seeing the results sunk me. A hairline fracture from the time I got bucked off a horse at my aunt's farm. Another hairline fracture from a skateboard accident in tenth grade. A chip in my L4 vertebra from a 1999 full-speed head-on collision in an April blizzard.

The chiropractor shook his head through his analysis of my results, tsk-ing with each new bit of bad news. He swam his finger along my backbone, pausing at deficiencies with less clear origins: degeneration midspine, curvature at the tailbone, my neck straight where it should curve, curved where it should be straight.

When I came home depressed about my future, Marty reminded me that I hadn't learned anything new. But the pictures of the irreversible damage — hard, clear, irrefutable images — left me feeling defeated.

When we arrive at the party cliffs, we stop. Most people come only this far, though two more lakes sit within easy walking distance. This first lake has the best diving and the best view, with the minimum expenditure of energy. But as soon as we come close to the clusters of people, Katie's light dims.

"Do you want to jump?"

Katie goes silent, studying her feet. In an instant, she's so transformed she cannot even say no. She shakes her head once, hard.

This Katie-transformation is less of a mystery to me now. I've recently read Susan Cain's *Quiet*, which has taught me to distinguish shyness from timidity or even introversion. Katie, who loves teasing her brother and jumping off cliffs and climbing dangerous rocks and dressing in outrageous outfits and shaving off her hair, is not timid or self-effacing. Katie, who joins everything from Girl Guides to ski racing to swim club to parkour to art classes to sleepover summer camps, is not introverted. Her preference of group activities (like Girl Guides) to solo ones (like reading) marks her as an extrovert. Why then is she shy? Cain explains in the simplest way: introversion is a preference for quiet, solo activities, whereas shyness is a fear of social judgment. When I read Cain's words, I remembered Katie's most consistent response to my questions about her shy behavior. "I'm scared," she would say, "that people will think I'm weird." Shyness is about fear. Introversion is about personality and preference. My Katie is afraid of social judgment.

"So what? It doesn't matter what people think," I say, willing myself to believe it, not just for my daughter but for myself. "Look at me, I'm weird."

"Exactly," she answers with her dimpled smile and lopsided hair.

It does not take us long to get away from the other people. After a fifteen-minute walk along a pebbly path, we arrive at the second lake, a more intense aquamarine with smaller rocks for diving. We have the whole lake to ourselves. Lively Katie returns. I haven't even gotten to the water's edge, when she yells, "I'm going in!" and pulls off her t-shirt and shorts, jumping up on a three-foot rock. Marty joins her in an instant, and they hold hands as he shouts "1-2-3 . . . Go!" They make a beautiful picture, Katie in her neon pink one-piece leaping into the air with an arm high above her head, her equally exuberant dad airborne at her side. I fail to capture the moment: I've abandoned my iPhone, imprisoned in the truck's glove compartment.

I didn't bring my swimsuit, thinking the water far too cold in June, but I can't resist the perfection. This view makes me thirsty for submersion. Not content to admire the splendor at a distance, I need to immerse myself in it, feel it, taste it. I strip down to my sports bra and underwear. As Marty and Katie shiver their way out of the water, I've got my toes curled around the edge of the rock and am doing my own countdown. I push hard and hold my breath as I dive headfirst into the frigid world. Cold grips me, but I don't leap out. Holding my breath against the freezing sensation, I take twenty quick, warming strokes to the center of the lake and then flip in a somersault before stroking more slowly back toward shore. I wonder why I don't come here more often.

When I climb out of the water, quickly grabbing my clothes, Marty holds his iPhone out to me: "Hey! Look! I got it! What a shot."

I don't recognize myself. He caught me midflight. My arms reach out over my head, shoulders strong, toes pointed. My legs hover above the ragged rocks while my torso stretches over the turquoise water, the lake's surface reflects off me, its shadows dancing along the length of my body. Having felt so weak since viewing my spinal X-ray, and so beaten down over the online pummeling, I let myself enjoy this image. The cliff-diving photograph makes me feel strong in the same way my unprecedented encounter with the cottonwood tree made me feel serene. Both sensations arrive unexpected, gifts from nature.

Bill Gaston's memoir *Just Let Me Look at You* has an alluring scene in which he's convinced that nature, via a gangly great blue heron, brings him omens about his dead father. Gaston ends the scene with the clunk of realism: "A belief that the world is communicating with you," he writes, "is seductive, but it's also a mark of schizophrenia." I take Gaston's point, but I do like to flirt with the ideas he has in play before he arrives at his practical conclusion. Isn't there an arrogance in believing we can understand, rationalize, and explain everything about the world beyond us?

"I don't know how I got that shot," Marty's saying. "I just held up my camera at the last minute. But I totally caught it."

I want to hang the photograph in my office or use it as my computer's wallpaper. I think of "Brave Katie" taped to Katie's mirror. This image will be my "Strong Angie." I would love to believe in this version of myself.

"Can we go now?" Ollie hasn't removed his backpack and crouches uncomfortably over the pebbles.

"Are you hungry, Ollie?"

I sit down and lean into the hot rocks, that warming sensation alone worth the brief discomfort of the frigid water.

As we eat our squished sandwiches, Marty tries to bring Ollie around with funny stories about bear spray. "Tourists heard the phrase 'bear spray' and assumed it worked like *bug spray*. So they put it all over themselves before hiking in the woods. Sprayed it on their tents and coolers and sleeping bags."

"They did not!" Katie laughs into her hand.

"Tip: it didn't work."

"No shit."

"Ollie — language. Anyway, bear spray can't really hurt you. It's made of oleoresin capsicum, residue from hot cayenne peppers." Marty slips easily into educator mode. "It's like what police use on people — pepper spray — but way lower concentration. Though you can shoot it farther, handy if you need it."

As the kids finish their treats, Marty palms his iPhone. "Cell service," he says, scrolling through the news feed.

"Oh god. This place just became a little less like heaven."

The old social media controversy about my memoir has again bubbled into real-world wrath. As a novelist, I am fascinated that people commit to a position without knowing the whole story, and that they do so based on personal allegiances rather than facts. Why not engage in dialogue? I wonder if the oversimplified and polarized (good versus evil) approach to controversy is new with social media? I certainly notice it more. Why do people feel confident judging someone based on a bit of information that a biased party provides in a Facebook post? What is it about that kind of easy condemnation that seems so thrilling and energizing to people, filling them with the intoxication of being right?

In a 2018 *Forbes* article called "Your Brain on Drama," health journalist Nicole Fisher explains that research on the ways in which social media and its drama affect the brain is still at its earliest stages. Nonetheless, scientists know that bonding with others, in teaming up against a shared enemy, releases oxytocin. When we demonstrate our allegiance to a group by denouncing an outsider, that group rewards us with positive attention, which in turn floods our bodies with the brain's most happy-making chemicals. That bodily reward encourages attention-seeking behavior, prompting us to pursue more positive affirmation in the form of Facebook likes and other social media comments. The 24-7 access to social media, with its promise of the nonstop excitement of belonging, teaches us dependence on this positive reinforcement. As soon as we do not get that kind of attention, we feel anxious, dull, depressed. How do we respond? We click on social media and easily alleviate our anxiety or improve our mood. Online drama activates the pituitary gland and hypothalamus, which secrete endorphins, supressing pain and inducing pleasure. In the words of Dr. Loretta G. Breuning writing for *Psychology Today*, "The happy chemicals feel so good that we use our big cortex to figure out how to get more." Opiates and heroin, the most addictive drugs, have been designed to mimic the release of these very same hormones and chemicals. It is no stretch, then, to say that people can become addicted to social media in the same way, and for the same effect, that people become hooked on opioids.

The way these new media shape human interaction and touch every part of life feels dangerous. I do not yet understand any of it well enough to help myself, let alone teach my kids.

In *What I Talk about When I Talk about Running*, Haruki Murakami shares stories about people not liking him. Personal hostility comes as an occupational hazard of the writing life. When we express our opinions, when we tell a story as we see it, we give readers an opportunity to see things differently and take offense. Murakami explains that though he understands why people do not like writers, his comprehension does not make the hostility of others any easier to handle. I folded that Murakami page into a swan. Rejection and hatred do hurt. Social isolation hurts. When amplified on social media, they hurt worse. If only we could keep that kind of aggression at bay as easily as we fend off the bears, with one of Marty's education sessions and a bit of watered-down pepper spray.

About ten minutes from the second lake, we find a clearing. Previous campers have patted down the grass. A well-used fire pit sits close to the water. Marty dumps all the canisters in a pile next to the ashes. "Okay, here's what we're going to do."

"I'm not —"

"*Ollie*. Just listen."

Marty widens his legs in a shooter stance, aiming the bear-spray nozzle at a large rock two feet downwind of him. Katie imitates him on the sidelines, a miniature Charlie's Angel. "Okay," he says. "The more time we spend in the wilderness, the greater the likelihood we run into trouble. With any luck, you'll never actually need bear spray, but in case you do, you have to know how to use it."

The kids have already had run-ins with bears, right at home in our wild-urban interface. Coming in the house after walking home from Guides at dusk, Katie looked completely shaken, pale and wide-eyed. A mother on Facebook had recently warned of a strange man in a truck calling out to young girls. That's what I thought: a man in a truck. "Are you okay?! What happened?"

"I saw a bear," Katie said, with an alarming vacancy, her eyes unusually wide. She told us she'd taken the dark path home instead of sticking to the lit road, and she found herself far too close to a mama and two cubs. The grown bear stood right up on its hind legs as Katie slowly backed away. "I tried to say *hey bear, hey bear, it's okay*, but I couldn't make any words. I did everything else right, though." Within a week, Katie, no longer rattled, explained to me: "A bear standing up isn't being aggressive or mean. It's just scared. They're more scared of us than we are of them."

Only two weeks later, Ollie, walking a few blocks home in the dark from a babysitting gig, saw "two big fluffy dogs" playing in the middle of the road. He'd been home for nearly half an hour before he even thought to tell me. "When I got closer, they were bears, not dogs." He laughed. "So I just turned off my flashlight and walked past them, far enough away not to scare them."

"Ollie!"

"What?" He shrugged. "It's fine."

I am a prairie woman with mountain kids. Their nonchalance gives me waking nightmares.

Maybe Ollie's lack of fear accounts for his impatience with his dad's bear spray tutorial. Ollie's probably right: likely he'll never need bear spray. But I know Marty. He has an idea in his head: to shoot off all the expired bear spray canisters, while making it fun and educational. Our marriage has taught me: a Marty-plan in motion stays in motion.

"Myth number one," Marty says. "Bears are unpredictable. Not really true. Bears read, and act on, *your* body language. Don't be aggressive, and they likely won't be aggressive either. You want to have bear spray ready, but don't use it unless you *need* it. Or else you'll get a harmless bear riled and put yourself in a worse situation."

"Then why are we even —"

"*Ollie.* Just listen." I wink at him. "It won't take long."

"In fact, it's even a myth that bears are dangerous. Humans have hundreds of encounters with bears every year and hardly any result in injury. So what you want to do first is identify yourself — say softly *hey bear, it's okay, I'm just leaving now.* Stay calm. Keep your hands in sight. Make yourself look big. As soon as the bear loses interest, back away."

Whenever I hear this talk, I think of Sid Marty's *The Black Grizzly of Whiskey Creek.* Just as some humans can be mean and unpredictable, so too can some bears be mean and unpredictable. That black grizzly, by Sid's account, was a real asshole.

Katie, the obedient student, looks up at her dad, performing her perfect bear-encounter routine, holding her hands out front, stepping slowly backward toward the hillside. "Hey bear, hey bear."

Ollie rolls his eyes.

"Bear spray is the last resort. *But* if you need it, it works. Even better than guns. Plus with guns — if it works, you've got a dead bear. Here all you've got is a gone bear. Bears and people alive and happy." Marty looks like a cop, his legs spread and his arms stretched out, muscles tense, shooting blasts of spray at the rock.

He's enjoying this more than anyone, but Katie bounces, keen to get her turn. "You want to aim at the head or slightly below. Be sure your spray doesn't blow in the wind over the bear's head — because then all you've done is pissed him off and invited him to charge. As soon the bear stops advancing and steps sideways — get out of there! Leave. Success."

Marty empties his full canister as he talks. "Some people say use the spray to make a wall between you and the bear, shooting in lines like this. Others say use short blasts, like this." He hands the second canister to Katie. "It can shoot sixteen feet. Five meters. So wait until the bear comes close enough, then shoot. Eight-second blasts. In a real situation, don't use it all. You might need more later. Today, though, we'll use it all. Have at 'er."

Katie takes a moment to get the hang of the gadget. She gazes down her long, skinny arms with one eye closed, squinting toward her target, and quickly arrives at empty.

I take two tries to get the feel for it too, but then I'm surprised how fast the spray is gone. "This was a good idea, Marty," I admit, thinking of our initial fumbles while getting a feel for how the thing works.

"Hmmph," Ollie says from the hillside, not stepping forward for his turn.

"Bud. Come on." Marty won't give up. "Just give it a try."

"But it's stupid. You just sprayed three cans. That's not what bear spray is for."

"Here's yours." Marty holds it out to him. "Over here. Now. I want to see that you can do it."

"No. Someone is going to come. Then what? The air is filled with bear spray. This is dumb."

"Nobody's coming."

I can't decide which one of them is more stubborn.

"Katie." I gesture at her to follow me. "Up here." We don't need to listen to the two of them squabble. I move us to a safer distance from Ollie's spray, assuming Marty will eventually win the battle. "Do you know about Dad's worst encounter with a bear?" Katie nods, but I keep talking anyway, hoping to distract her from contributing to Ollie's aggravation. Or maybe to stop myself from intervening. "He'd planned to bike over the mountains from Fernie to Waterton. He camped in the middle of nowhere the first night in his hammock tent. Remember the nickname for hammock tents?" Katie coughs instead of answering. "Bear burritos," I say. "Dad found out why! He woke in the early morning with a bear sniffing, right at his feet. He started yelling 'hey bear, hey bear' but saw he'd only made the bear more curious. A *talking* bear burrito!" I've got an itch in my throat but keep going. "So he got louder, and the bear backed away enough for your dad to jump out. Imagine him standing there in his long underwear with his bear spray ready to aim and fire 'You come any closer, bear, and you're in for a world of pain!' The bear left, but Dad said it was a cocky teenage bear." I rub the back of my hand across my nose, which has developed an odd drip. Katie coughs again. "The bear didn't leave in any hurry, and as it meandered away from Dad's campsite, it kept looking over its shoulder. Apparently, it had a real *screw you* saunter. It even took a bluff charge, just for the fun of watching Dad flinch. Dad's original plan was to bike into town, stock up on supplies, and then camp at least one more night on the way home, but he was so scared that he biked into Waterton for coffee and breakfast then sped all the way home in a single day." I can hardly get out the last sentence for the burn in my throat.

"Mom? My eyes hurt?" Only when I see the sensitive skin

around Katie's eyes flaring red and her nose running do I notice the burn in my own eyes. "Katie! Run!" I push her out ahead of me and follow on her heels, wiping the back of my hand against the tears running down my face. We race back over the slanted, pebbly trail at the water's edge, an awkward trot, with Ollie and Marty panting behind us.

"I told you this was a stupid idea!!!" Ollie yells from the back of the line. *"I. Told. You!!!"*

"The wind," Marty coughs. "It changed direction."

"Because that's what happens. It's nature. You don't —"

"Ollie." Marty and I say it together. I think I hear Katie, her skinny limbs flying at the front of our line, giggling.

We stop together shortly before the first lake, all huffing, the hilarity of our situation spreading across my family's faces. "Quality parenting, Marty," Ollie laughs. It's something Marty said to me once in an argument: *Quality parenting, Ang.* The kids have picked up the phrase as a favorite family joke. "I can't wait to tell this one. 'And so then my dad *made* me shoot my sister with bear spray.' Really good childhood memory." All trace of surly Ollie has disappeared. His and Katie's eyes glisten with this bit of fun.

"Ollie did say no," Katie laughs with her brother, wiping her snotty nose on the hem of her t-shirt. "Right from the start. You totally did make him, Dad."

Marty's lighter too, enjoying the change of mood, even if he's the joke's butt. The fog of annoyance that has had us in its grip all afternoon breaks away, cracked open by laughter. Marty puts an arm around each of the kids, who look a photographer's dream, skin golden in the perfect early evening light. Marty meets my eye and makes an expression I know well. If faces had sound, this one would go something like: *ooooof.* It's the laughing recovery after a spectacular ski fall. The twenty-something ski dude peeks through the adult mask: *Can you believe we're doing this? Parenting. And pulling it off too. I mean, you know, more or less. Most of the time.*

"Ang, grab a picture of us here by the lake. Me and my two dim kids who go around bear spraying each other."

"Dad! You're the one who —"

Ollie and Katie, on the same team at last.

Marty hands me his iPhone "All Bear Aware Hikers say cheese!" I snap the photo and rush the phone back to Marty.

"You've been thinking about that, haven't you," Marty asks, shoving the phone in his back pocket. "The social media stuff. I saw it on your face when we stopped to eat."

"Yeah. I was. But I had a realization. I hate being hated, obviously. It makes me sick. But walking down to the second lake, I thought, I don't hate them. All that hatred is on them, not me." Still silly from the bear spray mishap, I flutter my fingers above my head, all the hatred flying away, demonic butterflies freed.

I know from past revelations that I'll have to work at this one, not only to remember it, but to feel it. For now, though, that simple phrase — "the hatred is not mine" — lets me breathe. Having my direct portal to the hatred locked in the truck's glove compartment helps.

Ollie and Katie with their healthy young knees race down the last wet hill. Marty takes my hand as we make our way gingerly down the slope. "Make noise," I yell after them. "Bears!"

"Really, Ang? Bears? We're one hundred meters from the truck. People everywhere."

"Well, I worry."

"Yes, you do. Constantly."

He holds my hand over the first of the slippery rocks, but then lets it drop. When we started dating, I would take his hand on road trips, but he never let me keep it for long. "It's not that I don't want to hold your hand," he'd said. "It's just that it's uncomfortable for me. Physically, I mean." I believed him.

"Do you remember when I took Katie to that sport literature conference in Ontario, when she was only four months old? My mom traveled with us across the country to take care of baby Katie in the dorm room while I attended sessions." Marty has stepped in front of me on the narrow trail, and I curl my finger through his belt loop as I follow him. "Whenever I had a break, I raced back to our dorm room to check in and breastfeed. I was so stressed and nervous about everything." The defining feature of my approach to early motherhood? Anxiety. I worried constantly about what could go wrong, as if I'd taken on worrying as my primary job. "Toward the end of the conference, I confessed my all-consuming anxiety to a retired pediatrician, the wife of one of our most eminent, long-standing members. She looked at me with such kindness and said simply, 'Your attitude creates the attitude of your kids. If you see danger everywhere, so will they. Your job is to make them feel comfortable in — and curious about — the world. Not afraid of it. Relieve yourself of that burden of worry, and they will benefit.' So simple, right? But wise." Her advice helped at the time, gave me permission to quit worrying, to relax.

"I get what she means," Marty says. "As a parent, you model how to be in the world."

"Right. And in taking on what I thought to be the job of a good parent — to anticipate every potential danger to my children — I have modeled fear for Katie." I say it aloud to see if it sounds true.

I think it might be, at least in part. Katie's shyness comes from fear of social judgment; I have not modeled how to be unafraid.

"So what happened to that lesson?" The kids have come into view now, leaning against the truck in the setting sun. Marty pulls out his keys and unlocks the doors from a distance.

"I forgot it, I guess." Like all the most important lessons, remembering and re-remembering is a lifelong project.

"Could you do it, you think?" Marty turns to face me at the bottom of the trailhead, sliding his pack to the ground, with a musical clinking of empty canisters, and waits for my answer before joining Ollie and Katie at the truck.

"What? Not worry?"

"Yep, not worry."

"I'll try."

He cocks his head to the side and reaches toward my arm. He wants to believe me. "Promise?"

I lace my fingers through his and wonder if I can do it, relinquish the fear that I hold so closely. "I promise," I say slowly, "I really, really promise . . . that I will *try*."

Six

Peak-a-Week, Hijacked!

I spend the first weeks of our peak-a-week challenge attempting to compose a polite speech that will rid us of the boys. Could there be an adult, rational reason to insist upon a mother-daughter focus for these outings? Or do I simply want Katie to myself? The hiking itself goes fine. The peak-a-week goal does its job of getting us out the door and into the woods early each Saturday morning. The hikes help us appreciate the natural splendor of where we live. We do Castle Mountain first, mostly because it's a short hike, six kilometers return with just a five-hundred-meter elevation gain, and always earliest to be clear of snow, but it also has sentimental value.

Town has felt inhospitable since my return from a late June conference in France. I got home with a nasty head cold that I tried to minimize. Marty tends to resent the extra work shuffled to him during my absences, and I suspected he'd be annoyed by my returning in such a completely useless state. Still, I felt wretched.

On the second afternoon back, I heard a pack of boys playing with Ollie and Katie in the yard. When their play turned urgently loud, I peeled myself off the couch, digging my way out from under the snotty tissues, to investigate.

I squinted into the brightness, asked the rambunctious boys a few weak questions, and discovered that the older boys had wound up our two hyperactive puppies, Feist and Cassie, who we had acquired shortly after Blue's death in a fit of grief-induced insanity. Riled, Feist (the crazy sister) jumped on the youngest, smallest child. I scolded the puppies, calmed down the upset boy, watched him toddle down the road for his mom, emptied my nose into a Kleenex, and morphed back into the couch cushions.

Three minutes later my Facebook Messenger dinged. No *Hi Angie*. No words at all. Only a picture of two angry scratches on a boy's stomach. I propped myself up and started to type an apology. My phone dinged again: *I gather you're aware of this*. Again, I started to apologize, but a ding interrupted me. I reached for the NeoCitran, gulped the lukewarm liquid sugar, and read: *You shouldn't have children over until you train the puppies not to jump*.

Responses floated across the perma-screen in my mind's eye:
But I didn't invite the children over.
I didn't even know your kids were here.
I am SICK.

Instead, I addressed the mom by name and typed: *Oh no! I'm sorry. Poor boy. Please tell him we're sorry*. My remorse did not soften her. She did not acknowledge — never mind accept — my apology.

That afternoon, I went downtown to pick up an order from

a local shop. I'd requested the product months ago, but when it arrived, an employee had accidentally shelved and sold it. When I discovered the mistake, the store reordered. As I paid for the purchase, I asked the owner, "What's the usual process with orders? Would you have known to reorder if I hadn't noticed that someone else got mine?"

The owner disintegrated into tears, as stricken and bewildered as if I'd slapped her. "I don't know! I don't know what happened! I wasn't even here!"

I didn't understand. Not the tears. Not the defensiveness. Not the intensity. I didn't even care about the order, not really. I had what I wanted right in my hand. I asked the questions mostly to make conversation.

But I did — and do — care about the mystery of this confused way people read me, the shift in the way they interact with me. Can a Facebook post change a person? Can an out-of-context, misquoted representation of me alter how people perceive me and thus how I fit within my community? If someone says I am a mean-spirited bully, does everyone in that social circle begin to interpret my actions and words through that *bully* filter?

Does what we look for predetermine what we see?

I took my package and backed slowly away. As I left, the door chimes rang, the way they always did, but I felt unsolid. I had ceased to exist, a Facebook version of me taking my place. People saw, heard, and spoke to that construction of Angie instead of to me, to the way I felt on the inside. I floated above this Facebook-made Angie, watching, unable to draw a sensible connecting line from what I said or did to the way people reacted to me.

When I got home, I told Marty about the strange exchange, about the surprise of the crying. Perhaps I had already exceeded his current conflict quota. "You intimidate people," he said, grabbing his beer and heading for the garage.

Later, I sat in my office at my messy desk, pretending to write, and I listened to Marty apologizing to the neighbor down the street. Her children played in the quiet road, the little one unaffected by the day's earlier mishap with puppy Feist. Marty used the same words I gave our neighbor earlier. "We're so sorry!" "It's awful that the dogs hurt your son!" "We feel terrible." "We're trying to train the crazy puppies, we really are."

He got none of her bladed replies, none of her blame, none of her warnings. With Marty, the neighbor laughed, jovial. Through my window, I heard her smiling answers, her cheerful Southern drawl. "That's puppies!" "Our puppy was the same, a jumper." "Kids get hurt." "No worries!" "Thanks, Marty!" Theirs was a perfect summer evening encounter between friendly neighbors.

I sat immobile at my desk, listening to Marty and the neighbor laughing below, and I cried.

But I felt like a fraud too, recognized the performative aspect to my tears. Even as I let the liquid flow down my face, I also simply wanted Marty to come to my office and find me like this, to feel sorry for me. *Poor, poor Angie.* I wanted someone on my side to see the injustice, to see the pain, to see *me*.

I have waffled on my commitment to doing the peak-a-week hikes with Katie alone, and again we set out as a family of four. On the lush trail up Castle Mountain, all the aggravation of town's mini-antagonisms, real or imagined, evaporates, as does the self-pity that each slight inspires. A good experience in nature can release dopamine too.

"This is my home, *my Fernie."* I say it aloud, to the forest and the valleys and the rocky peaks, though I don't need the words anymore. Once I am in nature, I relax and feel like myself. Among these trees, I can now achieve a facsimile of the feeling I experienced with my cottonwood: cared for, a part of something much bigger than I am, at ease.

The blooms we usually see in June have finally appeared, now in July. Soapberries. Twinberries. Scarlet Paintbrush.

Marty and I are not the only ones with the idea of celebrating summer's late arrival with a brief, vigorous hike. The trail feels almost crowded, bustling with cheerful families. It's the most international crew of hikers I've encountered at home. I hear four foreign languages, three I recognize and one I don't. Our little town has found its spot on the tourist-destinations' map of the world.

"Your dad made me come here *winter* camping once," I say to Katie in a break from hello-ing other hikers.

"You?" She's adopted hiking poles to copy her dad and looks like quite the serious little trekker, a wide-brimmed hat shading her fair face. "You hate winter."

"I do. But we bought a super thermal sleeping bag. Dressed warm. Hiked all the way up to the top, on February fourteenth." I pause to see if the date registers, wondering if I'll get a *Gross! Romance!* from Ollie. "Under a full moon too. We were still just dating. The hike was so hard, breaking steep trail in the deep snow. For every five steps we took up, I slid three back. When we finally reached the top, sweating and freezing, your dad pulled out all these fancy supplies. Comfortable folding chairs. A miniature oven. Ingredients for gourmet pizzas. A bottle of champagne. Oysters. *Pillows* — like *real* feather pillows. I could tell he meant the expedition to be a big deal, so I tried to live up to all his fanfare, huddled in my sleeping bag, leaning toward the fire, eating all these treats, but eventually I got too cold, so I announced I was going to bed. He said, 'Wait. Come to look at the view. Just one more time.' He was all awkward and weird, but we walked out to the edge, and he started this stiff speech. 'When I look down on the lights below, I see the town where we will live together and raise a family —'" I wave my arm across an imagined Elk Valley, imitating an overly formal, nervous Marty and making the kids laugh, but Katie looks over her shoulder for her dad's approval. He's trekking along with his own poles and a wax canvas packer hat shading most of his face. Katie is clearly his mini-me. It strikes me that she's protecting him, making sure he's not hurt by our laughter. "Then he just stopped his speech," I say. "Stopped dead. Changed his tone and blurted: 'Forget it. I can't do this. I'm so nervous. Will you marry me?!'"

"Smooth, Dad!" Ollie laughs so authentically that he forgets to be a preteen grossed out by his parents' love story.

"Then what did she say, Dad?!" Katie looks less serious now, her smile digging its deep dimple into her left cheek.

"Well obviously she said yes," Ollie tells her, "or we wouldn't be here."

"I said 'In a heartbeat!' and 'Will I ever!' and then, just in case I'd been unclear, I added 'Yes! Yes! Yes!'" Remembering, I smile at Marty. "That's me. Angie Abdou: always playing super hard to get."

Katie studies Marty, questioning. Maybe she imagines him to be like the boys in her class, embarrassed by this display of girl affection.

Actually, he does look embarrassed. "Are you blushing, Martin?!"

His eyes skirt away from me, and he shrugs at Ollie. "I didn't propose on the cliff to be romantic," he says, holding out his palm with a tart thimbleberry for each of us. "I asked her there so that if she said no, I could push her off."

The joke delights Ollie and Katie, this venturing into adult terrain, this version of an Angie and Marty before Ollie and Katie. I feel I should speak against Marty's murder joke. I imagine a tweet about pushing reluctant brides off cliffs, the wrath the idea would provoke on social media. But the tweet would be without context. Ollie and Katie have context. They know Marty has no inclination toward physical aggression, spousal or otherwise. I don't need to tell my kids that murder and violence aren't funny. They know. They also know that Marty's words aren't really about murder, any more than Road Runner cartoons are about murder. Marty has simply made a joke to alleviate his discomfort at feeling exposed in the wake of my story about his grand proposal and his endearing blunder. Here, in the woods, with the smell of sunshine and dirt, with my grippy hiking boots hard on the trail, I have an easy time letting go of the externally imposed conscience of social media. With barely a thought, I decide to enjoy my family's laughter, inappropriate or not.

Why can I let go of the murder joke but not let go of the mother angry about her scratched son or the shopkeeper in tears because I asked a question about my late order? Society, with its squabbles and misunderstandings and grudges, has begun to wear on me. I keep a tally of each aggravation. One negative encounter that might be insignificant on its own grows and morphs into a pervasive pollution of negativity and judgment.

When I get into nature and away from society, I feel the separation. The pollution lifts. The air is fresh. I can breathe. My pulse slows. My brow unfurrows. I am not alone in this reaction. Scientific studies have proven that hiking is good for the brain.

Simply walking in wilderness decreases negative thoughts. In 2015, in the *Proceedings of the Natural Academy of the Sciences*, Gregory N. Bratman and his colleagues published an article called "Nature Experience Reduces Rumination and Subgenual Prefrontal Cortex Activation." Their data showed that ninety minutes in the wilderness, combined with turning off all technology, led to reduced neural activity in the area of the brain related to mental illness. In this work, as well as in a follow-up 2018 study, Bratman and his cowriters conceded that other factors (socioeconomic, psychological, physiological, environmental, genetic) can outweigh the positive effects of nature contact and that mental health issues are on the rise for many reasons (including an aging population, more sedentary lifestyles, and increased stress and loneliness); however, they asserted that the relentless move to increase urbanization and the resulting decrease in opportunities to immerse ourselves in nature rank high among the reasons for our growing troubles with mental health. Controlled laboratory studies reveal that simply seeing nature images and hearing nature sounds will decrease stress. Hikers in Bratman's studies reported that the act of trekking freed them from their own negative thoughts and gave them a break from their worries. They came back refreshed. Based on hikers' reports and physiological data, the study noted that urban hikers did not have that same restorative experience. Hiking in the wild releases the human mind from rumination. Urban hiking does not provoke the same peaceful lull in negative thought patterns. This work provides a strong argument for creating wild walking areas in urban centers to combat the increased levels of mental illness found in cities. The scientists noted a lack of certainty, though, about whether the decreased rumination came because of the immersion in wilderness or because of the break from technological distractions. I take the study results as expert permission to practice both, wilderness immersion and technological breaks, whenever possible.

A big red rock, visible from town, marks the summit of Castle Mountain. Throughout any regular day, I can point to the red cliff, especially striking in the evening sun, and say, "That's where Marty proposed." I don't pay attention to Castle Rock as often as I used to, rarely even think of the story. Hiking toward it now, I recall his nervous "I don't have money to buy a ring, but I have a strong back — I can bring all this up here; I can give you experiences." When he could, he has kept that promise.

The rock looks far away when we get started, as if we could never possibly *walk* to it. The kids grump when I point at our final destination, a red speck over the valley and through the forest and up the mountain. But they know the drill now, and we all keep trudging along, one slow step at a time.

"Watch, you'll see," I tell them. "It's not as far as it looks." This hike has an element of optical illusion, the way the red rock sneaks up. We're not there. We're not there. It seems like we will never, ever be there. Then, suddenly: we're there!

When we arrive, hikers already pack the summit bench, our favorite place to enjoy lunch, so we bushwhack around the top, find our own spot.

"Here's the fire pit where we camped."

"Here's the cliff where I proposed."

"Remember coming here when Ollie was obsessed with Stompin' Tom? He sang 'The Good Old Hockey Game' about five hundred times, while running circles around this tree."

"Katie, I think that was your first hike!"

Marty doesn't ask about my hiking book, and I'm relieved. Truth is, I haven't been writing much. The page has always been the place I go to figure out life, to worry my way through problems, to dump all those anxious words that flood my mind. Lately, I walk instead of writing. My walking works exactly the way scientists promise it will. As hiking lessens my rumination, my *need* to write also lessens. I head to the woods instead of to the words.

I do have a deadline, though. I also have certain professional obligations that necessitate writing. Plus, I teach writing, and if I don't ever connect with the page, how can I teach others to connect there? And, most simply, I have to write because writing is who I am. If I give up writing, I will need to find something else to do, something else to be, somewhere else to find meaning and lend structure to my existence. My dad's one piece of advice for life is simple: you have to know what you like, what you *really* like.

I really like the way I feel after I have written, when I have beaten the mess of life into sentences, into paragraphs, into chapters.

Once a month I see a woman. I don't know what to call her. A therapist of sorts. But she and I don't talk. Marty and I call the sessions my "breathing lessons," and other than that two-word description, I don't discuss my appointments at all, with anyone.

I knock on the door of the woman's basement apartment suite, and with minimal small talk, she leads me to a back room with two chairs and a massage table. Sometimes we sit on the chairs, facing each other, close our eyes, and breathe. Sometimes I go straight to the massage table. She moves my body around, and we pay attention to how I breathe. Afterward, we talk about how my breath felt, under her hands and in my chest.

I think the theory is that the body houses emotions, and her therapy (of bodywork, of touch, of breath) releases those emotions. I'm only guessing, though. She and I have never talked about how the whole practice works. She has offered no explanation. I'm surprised to find I like the break from words.

After she spends an hour touching my body and rotating my joints and lifting my limbs, all while listening to me breathe, she leaves the room for a few minutes. When she comes back, she always has a small glass, half full with tap water, no ice. She waits until I'm ready to open my eyes and sit up, and then she hands me the water. I am so relaxed I feel stoned, but eventually I speak, whatever sentence comes to mind. Then we have a brief, very brief, conversation about whatever I say. "Writing has been hard," I said recently. "It's not coming."

"What could you do?"

Always a keen student, I raced to produce a long-winded, fast-speaking answer about commitment and discipline and trusting the process.

She interrupted me with a laugh. "Or," she said, "you could just lie down. On the floor. Let yourself be carried."

I know the breathing coach's name, but I never think of her by it. In her life, she has had three different names. When she wants a new start — a new identity — she changes her name to one of her own invention.

I told her I envy her, that I often wish I could start over with a new name, get rid of the baggage of Angie Abdou, all the bad feelings and misconceptions and complicated histories that have attached themselves to those four syllables over the last fifty years.

"You don't need a new name," she said. "Just put those heavy emotions down. In the past. Where they belong. Leave them there."

In *No Mud, No Lotus*, Buddhist leader Thich Nhat Hanh goes against our communication-obsessed culture by advising that we should not tell our spouses what they have done to hurt us. By taking our negative emotions, formed by our self-obsessed interpretations of events, and hardening those emotions into narrative, we do not improve the situation. Thich Nhat Hanh says that by voicing these relationship troubles, we only *rehearse our grievances*.

I reread that page three times, let it really sink in that I don't always need to put my pain into words.

By taking my hurt feelings and turning them into a fully fleshed out story, I give them life and increase their power. Plus, while I take the risk of speaking because I hope to make myself understood and create a connection, my words might only deepen the divide between myself and others. I'm beginning to accept that words might not always have the positive power I have attributed to them. I suspect Marty, a man of few words, has always agreed with Thich Nhat Hanh's sentiment, intuitively. I remember when I tried to talk to Marty about the crying shopkeeper. "You intimidate people," he said, retreating to the garage with his beer. He's right to refuse me a stage for my soliloquies of pain.

As I tied my shoes at the breathing coach's apartment door, she recommended that I watch *Rebel in the Rye*, a movie about J.D. Salinger. The film documents Salinger's shift from writing with goals of fame and fortune, as he did initially, to writing for spiritual growth, which he did as a recluse for most of his life, though he completely ceased publishing his work. One line from the movie jumped out at me. I didn't have a pen and paper, so I jotted the words into my iPhone, as a text message to myself.

When my phone dinged, the disembodied query came as a surprise and a challenge:

Do you write to show off your talent or
to express what's in your heart?

For our next peak-a-week, we decide to undertake a more challenging adventure: Mount Hosmer. Guidebooks summarize it as a five-hour hike, nine kilometers, with a three-thousand-foot elevation gain. From town, it looks intimidating, all shadows and sheer rock faces. This hike marks the first time we set out not knowing if we will make it to the top. Mount Hosmer is a big, steep walk, especially for a ten-year-old child. "Let's just see how it goes," Marty says.

Marty and Ollie coming along has become the norm. I suspect they've all forgotten that this summer hiking challenge began with the aim of mother-daughter bonding time. I have no problem finding science to justify my urge for time alone with Katie. Research suggests that mother-daughter relationships affect future relationships more than any other. Analisa Arroyo of University of Georgia asserts that a poor mother-daughter relationship can lead to poor social skills and unhealthy attitudes toward eating. A mother's input shapes a daughter's self-perception, social competence, and mental health. In 2016, Fumiko Hoeft, Bun Yamagata, and their colleagues published an article in the *Journal of Neuroscience* arguing that the mother-daughter relationship, because of a similarity in brain structure, is the most important for determining how girls learn to process emotion.

Even with the backing of scientists to emphasize the importance of my developing a good relationship with Katie, I do not know how to say to Marty: "I don't want you guys to come. I want Katie to myself."

On the Mount Hosmer hike, our family pulls apart the way it often does: Ollie and I together, Marty and Katie together. Ollie sets a brisk pace and talks the whole way. I sneak glances back at Marty and Katie, with their hiking poles and their big-brimmed hats. They don't seem to talk at all. Their serious expressions match their serious trekking gear. Katie looks a bit sad and wan, but I assure myself she's just focused on the trail. That's the way she and her dad do things: with focus.

It rains on and off, leaving the trail mostly clear of hikers. We only cross two other couples the whole day. Ollie talks about Marvel films and YouTube's try-not-to-laugh videos and a sixth-grade schoolyard fight that a drive-by mom got on video and reported to the principal, but then the woman's daughter got the video and posted it online and the fight got more than a thousand views.

Most of the day, I barely know what he's talking about, my mind drifting in and out of his monologue.

"And then Jeremy was watching this video where they blindfold the girl and everyone takes her hand and makes her touch a part of someone's body and the blindfolded girl has to guess —"

"Wait. What? Is Jeremy allowed to watch whatever he wants?"

"Yeah. I guess."

"Do you watch these videos of . . . blindfolded people touching each other?"

"Sometimes."

"Maybe you shouldn't." The internet exposes Ollie to activities that never crossed my mind at his age. If not for the space this hike has provided, he'd likely never have told me about the blindfolded gropers. "You're an empathetic kid: you can imagine what it would be like to feel peer-pressured into that situation, especially if you really did *not* want anyone touching you." That's what the Harvard educators tell me, on a website devoted to teaching consent at every age: stress empathy and perspective in relation to personal boundaries.

"Yeah. I guess."

"If you have any questions . . ."

"Mom. I do *not* have questions."

"Well. If you ever do, let me know."

As we reach the last spot of level land before the push to the summit, Marty yells up for us to stop. While he collects sticks to build a fire in a small clearing just off the trail, I take the kids out to the mountain's edge and snap a few photos. The ground and foliage are damp, but by the time we return Marty has coerced his flame into catching. He crouches down, blowing, giving the fire oxygen to grow. I scroll through my photos. The clouds, which look dramatic and moody in real life, adding a dash of real outdoor adventure to the day, only look gloomy and dark in the pictures, the light unflattering.

"Did you get over being upset about the thing downtown?" Marty slides a bigger piece of wood into his pile of inflamed kindling. "The crying?"

"Yeah, I'm going to stop doing that. I promise. I've been thinking. Assuming everyone is mad at me all the time is narcissistic, as bad as assuming everyone loves me all the time. Why assume anyone is thinking of me at all? I'll stop. Really."

"Hmm." He doesn't believe me. "And when people do act like they're mad at you? You can ignore that?"

"Maybe they're having a bad day. Maybe they fought with their spouse. Maybe they're out of money. Maybe they don't like their new haircut. Maybe their emotion has nothing to do with me. I'm going to go with that."

"Okay," Marty says, a skeptical drag to his syllables. "Good idea." He hands me a sharp stick, and we all crouch around the small fire, roasting hotdogs. Marty pulls over a log for the kids to sit on, but I don't mind the ground and stay crouching.

When a young couple comes close to us on the trail, I feel guilty. I've been conditioned by a string of dry summers. "Are you sure we're supposed to be doing this?" Despite my brave speech, I'm still worrying about what people might think, about who might be angry.

"What? Eating?"

"The fire. I worry they're going to say something."

"Ang, it's raining. We'll make sure the fire is all out. We're fine."

Katie and Ollie hardly talk over lunch. They're tired. It shows in the droop of their bodies and the fall of their faces. A recent article in *Outside* magazine argued the importance of challenging kids, to give them experiences of being uncomfortable, that there is, in the words of famous climber Alex Honnold, more to life than being cozy. Probably that's true, but I hope Ollie and Katie will find the summit worth the effort and discomfort.

Marty creates a lunchtime make-work project for himself. He whittles notches into sticks with his fancy new pocketknife and then leans the sticks into each other. He sets the contraption near the fire and hangs his outer layer close to the heat. "Want me to dry your jacket, Ollie?"

"No."

"Want to try my axe and cut us some more firewood?"

"No."

Katie curls in on herself, close to the fire, an antisocial posture.

With my knees sore from crouching, I signal her to slide down the log to make room for me. I hold my hands up to the warmth before speaking. She does not interrupt the quiet. After a few still moments, I set my warm hand on her knee. She wears bright purple pants. A rain jacket covers her t-shirt, but I know it's purple too. It says *beautiful*, broken into three syllables down her torso: *BEAU- TI- FUL.* Finally, I ask her simply, "Are you okay?"

She nods. "Yep." She doesn't take her gaze off the end of her stick, her hotdog slouching above a flame.

"You seem a bit sad."

"Nope." She rotates the charred side of the hotdog toward the sky. "Just tired."

I put a finger on her chin and turn her face toward mine. "You'd tell me if anything's wrong? You do seem sad today."

"I'm not."

I come in and out of thinking about Katie's shyness: *she's getting better; maybe she's not; she seems fine; maybe she isn't; she doesn't have an issue; maybe she does.* Yesterday, my mom told me that she and Katie were gardening in the front of the house when a couple, my parents' friends from down the street, stopped to visit. "She wouldn't even talk to them, Angie. Not even look at them. I told her, 'Katie! You have to at least try!'"

I responded not with anger, exactly, but definitely with heat. "Mom, *you* are shy. If anyone should understand, you should."

My mom's advice came from a place of deep concern and admirable intention, I know that, but our brief conversation made me aware of the weighty expectations we all pile on Katie. In one of my earliest memories, I was maybe four or five years old, I attended a fair with my family. My parents paid for my brother and me to go into a bouncy castle. I knew what they meant for us to do. We should jump and laugh and make a great show of having fun. But I didn't want to jump or laugh. Instead, I sat at the outer edge of the castle, my back pushing against the fabric wall, my body sinking into the floor. I watched the other kids jump. As the clock ticked down on the bouncing minutes that my parents had bought for me, they tried to catch my eye. They gestured and mouthed instructions at me. *Jump! Play! Get up!* I sat, paralyzed. The more I knew what they wanted me to do, the less I could do it. The buzzer went, and all the happy, sweaty kids filed out. I followed them, burning with the shame of my failure to be what others expected me to be: their idea of a happy, normal kid.

"You just sat there! The whole time!"

"We paid for you to jump! All the other kids jumped!"

I could not have explained my behavior then, but now I would say that the stage of the bouncy castle, the performance it required of me, turned me off. I didn't want to act. I didn't want to jump and laugh, for anyone.

By the fire, I tell Katie the story. "Do you ever feel that way?"

She doesn't answer. I wait. Marty has convinced Ollie to try the axe. He cuts a small branch into bits of firewood, carries them over, and places them in the embers at our feet.

"Kind of, yes," Katie says finally. "Maybe. More like I think if I don't talk and I don't look at people, they will forget I exist."

The thought of a world in which Katie does not exist hurts my heart. "Why would you want that?"

"I guess, like you say. So that I don't do the wrong thing or not say the right words."

Oh my god, she's a little mirror of me. I have spent two full years obsessed with people mad at me for having said the wrong

words or having done the wrong thing. "Sweetie. You can do whatever thing and say whatever words you want. Your own Katie way."

Poet Philip Larkin said it best: "They fuck you up, your mum
and dad. / They may not mean to, but they do."

Katie pushes a big chunk of hotdog and bun in her mouth and
then laughs, tight-lipped with her cheeks stuffed full.

"I think if you stay too quiet, your behavior has the opposite
effect of what you want. The shyness doesn't draw people's attention away from you. It draws their attention toward you. Because
they worry about you."

She nods once.

"I love you."

I watch while she chews and swallows. How hard should parents push? Belonging to society does require *some* performance.
"Yeah I know," she says, and then, as an afterthought, she adds, "I
love you too."

We have an easy walk from lunch to the summit. The view at
the top fills me with awe. We can see forever, from the top of the
world. Fear flutters in my chest as we get close to the edge for
photos. The images will be magazine-worthy.

"You did it, Katie!"

"Ahem!"

"You did it too, Ollie. Great job, guys. *This* is a *real* hike. Look
at us!"

The height, the rocks, the steep drops below us — all of it
so utterly gorgeous. "Be careful, kids!" Marty does not mock my
warnings. A fall in the wrong spot here would mean certain death.
Ollie and Katie cooperate for the photos, posing with each other

and with each of us. Perched on cliffs above sheer rock faces, they smile joyfully for the camera.

Getting here is a real accomplishment. I think the kids know it. They look proud. They forget to bicker. They don't turn to Marty for the typical mountaintop treats. Our arrival seems reward enough. We rest on rocks, without speaking, and stare down at the clouds.

I've hauled my current Knausgaard book along on the hike. I'd been tweeting about the project of reading all of Knausgaard's *My Struggle* series, so I thought it would be fun to get a picture reading one of them on a mountain peak. I am at the part of the story where his family has begun reacting to the first book, threatening to sue him. Right before publication, he sends the manuscript to his brother, wanting approval but knowing the push to publication will not stop, no matter how his brother reacts. Karl Knausgaard will, if he must, pick publishing the books over keeping a relationship with his brother. Still, he sends *My Struggle* by email and waits for the brother's response. And waits. I know his stress, his preoccupation, his despair, his impatience. Finally, his brother replies, in an email, with the subject heading: *Your Fucking Struggle*.

My stomach clenched when I read that. *Your Fucking Struggle.* I felt ill with nerves for the author. I know that particular sickness well, the fear of disapproval, the sting of rejection, the vulnerability of the exposure that comes with releasing personal words into a public world, and the threat of being outcast for expressing private thoughts and feelings. I never want to experience that feeling again. Yet I also know I cannot write if I am afraid of it.

When we decide we're ready to descend, I expect Katie to take off, rounding the switchback corners like a race car driver. But each of her movements drags lethargically. After a few steps, she stops to take off her pack, puts it on again, stops to adjust her shoe, takes two more steps, stops for a drink of water.

"You can drink *and* move," I say. "That's the beauty of a CamelBak."

"How far is it? Until we're done?"

"Well. It took us four hours to get up here," I say. "You know where our truck is. We're going back the exact same way. How long it takes depends on how fast we walk."

"I'm tired."

"We can have rests. But we only just started. We have to walk before we rest."

"I'll go with her," Marty says. "You go ahead with Ollie."

"No, it's okay. I'll go with her. Sorry, Katie. You set the pace. I'll follow. Do you want a treat first?"

"Really, Ang. I'm happy to walk with Katie. You run up with Ollie. He's getting too far ahead. We are good." *We.* Marty is as protective of Katie as she is of him. They make a good team.

I go. Father-daughter relationships must be important too.

Linda Nielsen, writing for the Institute of Family Studies, argues that we too often overlook this particular parent-child relationship, placing more emphasis on father-son and mother-daughter bonds. However, her research indicates that well-fathered daughters perform better academically than those with poorer relationships with their dads. Girls close to their fathers also tend to secure higher career satisfaction and report emotionally intimate and fulfilling relationships with romantic partners. Nielsen insists a daughter's relationship with her father is actually more important than that with her mother in determining happiness and success, in ways ranging from avoiding mental illness and poor body image to refusing to be "talked into" sex before she feels ready to demonstrating good goal-setting abilities and prioritizing her own needs. Dr. Marie Hartwell-Walker, writing for Psych Central, concurs: "Children really do learn what they live." A father who treats his wife and his girls well teaches his daughters what to expect from men. Katie is lucky to have Marty as a dad. He sets her up for life with an excellent example of how men should treat her.

Ollie chatters his way down the mountain, in a cheerful mood after his impressive summit, the effortful part of the day behind him. "You know how I do movie reviews for my YouTube channel? Well I've been thinking of writing my own movie scripts. I keep starting and throwing them out. I don't really think I can be a screenwriter. I just don't have any original ideas."

"Ollie! You're twelve!"

"Yeah but every idea I come up with . . . there seems to already be a movie kind of like it."

"First of all, you're twelve." I watch my footing, leaping over roots. He moves so fast I must be careful not to trip. I have a habit of focusing on the conversation instead of the trail and arriving at the bottom with bloody knees.

"Yes, I am twelve. You already said that."

"Okay, second of all, some people would say there are no new movie ideas. Only new takes on the same old stories. Nothing new under the sun. You'll have your own Ollie spin, and *that* will make your movie a new idea."

"Ollie spin? Riiighhhht. I sure hope you have a *third-of-all*."

"Third of all, you're *twelve*. Look. I'm a writer. I get paid to write. Some people like my books. And I can tell you that you are light-years ahead of where I was at twelve. Maybe . . ." I ruffle his hair, ". . . don't give up just yet."

He brushes my hand away and makes a noncommittal sound in the back of his throat. *Hmmph.* The dark clouds have moved in again and the sky spits. I pull Ollie's rain jacket out of his backpack and hand it to him.

I keep looking behind us to check on Marty and Katie. I sporadically see them on the switchbacks above, but they make halting progress. I wonder if Katie has ended up hurt or if the hike is simply too much for her, but Ollie refuses to wait. We stop a few times, sitting on fallen logs to rest, but within moments, he's antsy and keen to go again.

"Can I tell you about a crazy book I've been reading?" I don't know how interested he'll be in the ideas, but we've got some time to kill, and I want to try putting my thoughts in words.

"Sure."

"So I've been looking for a writer who explains this sense I get in nature, when we're hiking, where I feel more purely myself. Like not so taken over by worries or by what I imagine other people say or think about me."

"Uh-huh?"

"And I like the ideas of this woman called Iris Murdoch, a philosopher and a novelist."

"Novelists can be philosophers?"

"Actually people mostly see her as a novelist, I think. But this book of hers I like from 1970, called *The Sovereignty of Good*, is philosophy. She writes about the power of nature and art, of anything truly beautiful, to pull us out of ourselves. She claims that self-knowledge is a delusion. Humans, so prone to anxiety, create this kind of veil of delusion, which blocks our true understanding of the world. Our self-focused worries distort reality."

"Wow." Ollie pulls on a branch as he walks so it snaps and hits me, where I follow behind him. I've never heard anyone fill the word *wow* with such boredom.

"Okay, smart ass. Not so fascinating to you. I get it. But I think you might relate to this part: Murdoch says anything that can pull our attention outward is connected to virtue. The beauty of the natural world is good simply because it frees us from that anxious obsession with self for a moment. So nature makes us better people, less preoccupied with our own troubles, more outward-looking."

I search up the mountain, and I don't see Marty and Katie at all anymore. I wonder if they've stopped for another break, the divide between us growing.

"Do you ever feel that way," I ask Ollie, "like if you get lost in your admiration of nature, you can forget all of the silly stuff you usually worry about?"

"Ah . . . nope."

"That's not true, though." I unzip my jacket, wishing the day's weather would make up its mind. "What about Juan de Fuca? When you were looking at the ocean? I remember the way you said *amazing*. You lost yourself in that view."

"Okay. Maybe. Juan de Fuca was pretty cool."

"Iris Murdoch calls that feeling 'unselfing.'"

He doesn't say anything for a while, and I leave us to walk in silence, wondering whether I'm ridiculous to expect him to be interested in these ideas. "Do you think," he finally asks, "that's what happened with Your Tree? The god-y one in the backyard? You got unselfed?"

"Ollie. Wow. Yeah, maybe." I have never thought of my cottonwood tree in the context of Murdoch. "Like staring at the tree out my window took me away from myself so much that I felt almost out of body . . . or inhabited by something other than myself." Giving my attention over to the tree was such a complete contrast with my state for months, weeks wasted with me completely possessed by social anxiety and petty squabbles. "You know what — yes, I think that was unselfing, like an unselfing so I could reself, or something, but yes."

I remember the picture of me cliff diving, my admiration that originally seemed so ego-driven to me. I liked the photo because I looked strong. But I also responded to the image because I looked at one with nature, hovering over the cliff, the water reflected on my torso. If I imagine the picture as a jigsaw puzzle, I could pop out the one piece with my body and substitute a piece of sea green to match the water — it would be like I was never there. It could be one hundred years before or one hundred years later. Me: irrelevant. In the photograph, I'm at one with nature, but I am also small and trivial in relation to nature. The image — the surprise of it — did take me out of my anxiety and help me escape what Murdoch calls "the brooding self."

I would like my children to have that kind of relationship with nature — treasuring it as a space that gives the mind a holiday from this complicated life, the perplexing strain of human relationships.

Ollie and I get to the truck well before Marty and Katie. We search for thimbleberries to reward them with when they finally finish.

"Oh man. She is not going to be happy. It's taking them so long."

"Yeah. Well it is a pretty long hike."

I forgot to get the keys from Marty. We're locked out of the cab, but Ollie and I stretch out in the truck bed, using our packs as pillows. It must be almost dinnertime, but the sun feels warm, and I enjoy the sensation on my bare legs. When I see the trees wiggling up in the distance and then spot a little red head, I yell, "Woohoo! Way to go, Katie!" Ollie and I cheer enthusiastically as Marty and Katie descend the last fifty meters to arrive at the truck. Marty holds his hands over his head triumphant, wearing the big smile he reserves for athletic success. Katie copies his victorious pose, but only for a moment before plopping her pack on the ground and climbing into the backseat.

"That was great, Katie! You did it! That's a long hike."

"Yep. It was pretty hard." She leans her head against the window and within minutes falls fast asleep.

The dirt road back down to town weaves and turns and bumps. Soon it lulls Ollie to sleep too. The non-existent shoulder and deadly drop into the valley below keep me from relaxing at all. I work up my courage and tell Marty that next time I want to go hiking without him and Ollie. "I was hoping to have more time alone with Katie." It's hard to say aloud because I love Marty and I love Ollie and I love doing things together, but I simply want to spend some days with my full attention on Katie.

"Because of your book," he says.

I hear it as an accusation. "No." Marty and I have gotten better at backing away from fights but not always better at engaging in discussions that include judgment or conflict or even a difference of opinion. I work to keep my tone even. "Not because of my book. Because of Katie."

He nods, and we drop it.

The wish to give the hikes a mother-daughter focus might seem a small thing. I could have chosen not to push for it. I could have adjusted my focus to a summer of family hiking. That would've been an easy compromise.

Easy is the right word. It's *easy* to let our plans be hijacked. And not only our small plans. How often do we compromise in order to align with what we imagine family, friends, colleagues, employers, and society want us to do, to think, to be? We perform our selves instead of being ourselves. Our relationships, our lives, our very selves can be hijacked by the expectations of others, as we perceive them.

Katie and I had a simple plan: a mother-daughter attempting to climb a peak-a-week. I would like to do a few of those hikes, alone together, before the always-too-short summer ends.

When Marty pulls to a stop in front of our house, the kids stir awake. I hold out a hand for Katie, helping her down to the driveway. It's a bit of a jump, and she's groggy. I catch her limp warm body in a hug as her feet hit the ground. "Mom?" She rubs her eyes and then holds up her arm to shelter her face from the sun. "Next time . . . next time, do you think, maybe, can just you and me go on the hike?"

Did she hear our conversation? I don't think she did. She seemed fast asleep. "Yes." I smile, but I do not try to explain to Katie how much this time will mean to me. There's no way for her to understand, not until she has her own children. "Yes, Katie, we can absolutely go hiking, just you and me. I would like that."

As simple and true as a sentence can be: *I would like that.*

Seven

A Hike of Our Own

"Rise and shine!" I flip the light switch. A lump on the top bunk stirs and groans. *"Katie Camper Super Duper!* Up and at 'er!"

"Agggh. Mòm, I'm so tired." Katie's red hair splays across her Ariel-themed pillowcase. She squints, annoyed, and then drags the pillow over her head.

"Hey, here's a good deal. If you get up quick, I won't say a word about the state of your room." I cannot imagine a messier child, this small space a testament to her many interests: crafts, fashion, writing, slime, cards, magic, reading, swimming, formulas, Guides, board games, seashells, costumes, rocks, jewelry, feathers, hats, . . . cardboard boxes? Her room gives me heart palpitations. "Let's go! Let's go! Let's go!" I turn up the volume on my enthusiasm to compensate for my own fatigue. We had friends over last night, and we all stayed up too late. The clock had snuck past 10:30 before I finally chased Katie to bed.

The lump on the bed does not move.

"Okay. I'll put on my coffee and get your breakfast ready. I'm coming back in fifteen to find an up-and-dressed Katie Hiker Super Duper."

But after I drink a cup of coffee and set out a bowl of cereal with a banana, Katie's room is still quiet, her red hair and her Ariel pillowcase completely disappeared under her comforter. I flip her light off and quietly open the door to my bedroom. I like to sleep with the blinds halfway open so that when I first wake, I see the big cottonwood tree, but I find the room pitch black. Marty has gotten up after me and pulled all the blinds shut to enjoy a rare sleep in.

I sit down on the edge of the mattress, next to his body. He radiates heat. He flings a heavy arm across my lap. "Come back to bed," he says into his pillow, his voice thick with sleep.

"I wanted to do this hike," I say, lacing my fingers through his, "but Katie's not keen. I can't get her up."

Marty rolls on his side and snakes a hand up under my shirt, rests it on the bare skin of my lower back. The heat feels good. *Healing hands*, he always says. "Mm. It's the weekend. Let her sleep." He still doesn't open his eyes.

"Yeah, but," I toy with his fingers in my lap, "I feel like I'm the only one sustaining any interest in my hiking plan."

"Well. It is *your* hiking plan." He slides to the middle of the bed, making room for me.

"Yes, it is my plan, but I thought . . . well I thought we were all into it."

Instead of responding, he tugs on my arm, pulling my body into his. "Come back to bed," he says again.

It's Saturday. The room is dark. The house is quiet. The kids are sleeping. My husband is warm. I go back to bed.

"Sleepy head! It's eleven o'clock!" I point at Katie's pyjamas. I have had my return to bed, risen to drink two more cups of overcooked coffee, eaten a bowl of plain yogurt with blueberries and flaxseed, packed our hiking gear, and called Katie seven times. Finally, she's downstairs, but still not ready. "You don't want to come, do you?" I put my hand on her pillow-flattened hair. "It's okay. You know what — I'll go alone."

"Are you sure?" Katie squints up at me, almost a flinch. She makes this face whenever she worries someone will be mad at her. "I feel bad."

She's grown this summer, both the legs and arms of her pyjamas now too short. Sometimes I catch a glimpse of adult-Katie in her fair child's face. Soon she will ask me to replace the Ariel bedsheets. "Yep, I *am* sure. Don't feel bad. It's the weekend. You're not in the mood. That's fine. Call a friend over to play this afternoon, and I'll see you at dinner."

Thirty minutes later, I'm in the garage, doing one more check before I head out. With the late start, I've chosen a mountain I can do in a few hours, but one with a steep uphill for maximum outlook in minimum time. In Lori Lansens's mountain novel, a character says the uphill is good for our *character* and the view is good for our *soul*. Today's hike will have a bit of both. I tend to underprepare, especially for short hikes, so remind myself to bring some snacks and enough water. The afternoon does not have to be a sufferfest.

"Mom?" Katie peeks into the cluttered garage, a testament

to all her father's interests, and just as likely as Katie's bedroom to provoke my heart palpitations. She wears denim camo shorts, folded above her knee, and a fitted blue tank top. Her legs look long and strong. "Can I still come? I want to."

"Really?" I worry her only motivation is a belief that I want her to come.

"Yes! Totally! I do!" She excels at the art of pleading, though usually she uses her talent to get Dairy Queen ice cream after the ski hill or candy bags at the movie. "Please," she says, giving the word three syllables.

"Sure! Of course. Come! Grab your CamelBak, let me get extra sustenance, and we're off. Resume project Smoke and Fire." Katie grins, knowing sustenance to be the code word for treats.

"Not exactly a dawn start," I say as we hit the trail. I look at my watch. "Noon. That's fine. Even if we take six hours, we'll be back by dinner." When Katie decided not to come, I picked a mountain I thought I could summit and return in three hours. We'll take longer now, but I am happy to have her at my side. "It's hot. Wait up." I grab Katie by the tail of her shirt and spray another dash of sunscreen on the back of her neck and the tops of her shoulders. I love the summer heat, but worry about my fair-skinned girl.

She does not like the trail's steep grade. Almost immediately, she's flushed, overheating in the midday sun. She lifts the hem of her tank top to wipe sweat from her face. I chatter to distract her, asking questions about her friends at school and swimming. She tells me stories about who was fighting with whom last term and who likes whom and what so-and-so did to get in trouble. I recall all the days I've asked, "What happened at school?" and gotten

"Nothing" in reply. I do not take her words for granted. Walking loosens lips.

After an hour, she goes quiet. I try to keep luring her along with gummy bears and red licorice. We're only halfway up when she announces she wants to turn back. "I'm so sleepy," she says. "Please, can we stop."

"Katie, the thing with hiking, with any sport, is that you will always want to quit at some point. If you give yourself the option of stopping, you'll *always* stop. Do you think you can push on? We'll rest in half an hour, for lunch. You'll love this one at the top. It's so beautiful. I promise."

Katie has stalled on the trail, midstride, one leg uphill from the other, her hands tucked into the straps of her backpack, her chin hanging low. "I want to quit," she says quietly. "I just want to go home." She aims the words at her boots. "But now I feel guilty."

Well. I don't want my girl to feel guilty. "Do you remember my friend Jon Turk?" I lean into a spruce tree and watch Katie swing her head once to indicate no. "He goes on these epic adventures and writes about them. He breaks records for trekking to places that nobody has trekked to, for paddling solo across oceans that no human has crossed, for circumnavigating islands that nobody else has circumnavigated. The reason nobody else has circumnavigated them? Because they are completely inhospitable to human life." Katie lifts her eyes to peer up at me from under her long bangs, maybe a little bit curious about nutty Jon Turk. "You can imagine how often *he* wants to quit, when he's cold and hungry and tired and alone — but if he quits, he will die. He has a saying: 'When the going gets tough, the tough make tea.' When I am tired, I picture him, crouched in the ice, surrounded by polar bears, far from civilization, drinking his cup of tea, finding the energy to go on. *Or die.*" I say the last two words dramatically, hoping for a laugh.

"We don't have tea," she says, offering a small smile.

"Oh, but we do! Sometimes your mom surprises you!" I have never before made tea for Katie, but I copied this trick from Marty, who uses a little earl grey with milk and sugar to urge his girl along on early ski mornings. I pull a thermos from my bag and pour the steaming liquid into the lid, set it on a stump, and gesture for Katie to have a seat on the ground. "Let's stop and have a treat, then see how we feel."

I lay out a blanket on the forest floor and we both crawl onto it, leaning into a stump, dipping carrots in hummus. "Nice treat, Mom," Katie laughs, the food injecting some new energy into her. She loops her carrot around in the hummus and lifts a big dollop toward her mouth.

"I have a real treat too. After the carrots." The sunlight coming through the cedar branches hangs golden in the air, reminding me of a Laura Nelson painting. "Here's something neat. One of my favorite artists loves these forests, so she makes art inspired by them. After seeing her paintings, I see the forest differently too. Think of this: Laura sees the forest, makes a painting inspired by that seeing, shows the painting to me, and then when I am back in the forest I see the same trees I've always seen but in a new way, as if through the eyes of the painting." I don't know what I'm trying to say exactly, something about the power of realism to make us see the world around us in a new and deeper way. When I praised Laura for the evocative, stirring beauty of her trees, she replied simply: *The forest is my church.* "I never admired the way the light comes through the trees here until I saw it in Laura's work."

"It is pretty," Katie says, her eyes rolled skyward as she slurps up the last of her tea. "The flecks in the air. Like fairy dust. Or little jewels."

"And now, a treat!" I reach into my pack, drawing out the surprise. "Unless you don't like chocolate," I add. "Then I'll have it. I'll trade your chocolate for my share of the carrots."

"I do like chocolate! You can have *my* share of the carrots!" She giggles and pushes the Tupperware my way.

I set an entire chocolate bar in front of Katie and lie back on the blanket, lifting my face to the light beams. "Have you ever heard about forest bathing? We had Japanese exchange students before you and Ollie were born, and they told us about it — doctors actually prescribe time in nature to cure sickness. Like, you could be rundown, stressed, and burned out, and you'd get a doctor's note for two days' hiking in the national park. I'd forgotten, but I've been reading a book called *The Nature Fix*. It says Japan has forty-eight official 'forest therapy' trails. Some people say nature even works like a miracle drug. Kills cancer cells."

"Hmm." Katie breaks her bar up into squares, organizing the candy into some system that only she understands. The bits of chocolate form an intricate pattern on our blanket. "I think the trail that just me and you did last time would be better for forest bathing. This one doesn't feel like . . . well for me, this hike doesn't make me feel *better*." Her cheeky smile presents her words as a challenge. "Not exactly."

"Funny girl. This one *is* a bit too hard, hey? Maybe we should have waited a few years for our hiking goal. Last weekend *was* fun, I agree." On Sunday, I took Katie on an easy walk through an old-growth cedar forest. The whole trail took a little over an hour and had minimal elevation gain. We lollygagged and played amongst the giant trees, climbing on logs, tucking our bodies into caves hollowed into enormous trunks. I took pictures of Katie, so tiny and perfect, like a miniature fairy in this otherworld of forest. "Yes, that forest *was* medicine, the whole afternoon a miracle cure. Now that you say it. That hike felt the same to me too."

So why am I dragging her up another mountain this weekend?

The Nature Fix advocates for the importance of children developing an early relationship with nature, explaining that E.O. Wilson believed that the best window for learning biophilia is before adolescence. I am beginning to wonder if this peak-a-week goal works to form the kind of relationship E.O. Wilson had in mind. Katie is right, about last weekend and the joy of immersion in nature *without* the push to summit. Maybe today only teaches her to see nature as an adversary, an obstacle to overcome, a challenge to conquer, or even (I hate to admit) a punishment to endure. If I ever manage to break away from my lifelong commitment to the difficult, I might have to credit Katie as my teacher. "There's a 'Happy Train' in South Korea that takes school bullies to a natural park for two days," I tell her, "so they can learn to be nicer."

"We should send Ollie on a happy train." She screws the lid back on her empty thermos and tucks it into my pack.

"It's the green that makes forest therapy effective." I ignore the dig at her brother. "Even a picture of nature hanging in a work office improves happiness." A research study conducted at the VU University Medical Center in Amsterdam monitored participants' stress levels as they completed math problems; afterward they looked at two sets of photos — one urban, one wild. The photos featuring green flora activated the parasympathetic nervous system, triggering rest functions and reducing stress. "A neighborhood with buildings *painted* green has less crime than neighborhoods without."

"What? You're lying."

"Nope. I am only paraphrasing. *The Nature Fix*. If it's a lie, it's not mine."

By the time we finish our snack, Katie looks more cheerful and agrees to keep pushing upward. The optimism and energy prove short-lived. Within five minutes of walking, she asks how much farther to the top. She must hear the whine in her own voice because she adds, "Sorry. I'm not fun. This is supposed to be fun, and I'm making it no fun."

"Oh Katie! You're the funnest girl I know."

"But I just . . . I don't like hiking anymore." She has tears in her eyes when she says it.

In the spring, I had dinner with Randall Maggs, a famous hockey poet. I told him our family's plan to hike the Juan de Fuca Trail. With his kids long grown and now raising children of their own, he responded from a place of experience. He seemed both envious and skeptical of the hiking plan. "Do your kids know that feeling," he asked, "of not being able to go on but *having* to go on?"

I look at Katie on the trail today and think *now* she knows it.

I can almost see the peak when Katie flops at the side of the trail, crying. "I want to go home."

Crying makes my skin ache. My scalp tightens. My veins hurt.

I cannot explain my aversion to sobbing children, but I can't deny it either. Whenever I hear crying, I want to squeeze my eyes shut, cover my ears, and yell, "Stop it! Stop it! Stop it!" I *hate* crying. A woman named Desi — a reader and thinker I admire — criticized my War on Crying as represented in *Home Ice*. The parenting strategy she proposed instead? Simple: let kids cry, especially in sports. She says, "Crying hard is trying hard," and there is nothing wrong with big emotions.

I try to learn from Desi and not be so derailed by these over-wrought and noisy displays of sadness. Partly, my frustration with tears stems from my inability to decode them. I do not know what they require of me. Is this hiking-trail breakdown the right kind of sporty tears? The "crying hard, trying hard" ones that we push through to reach a goal? Or are they ones that show I've already pushed too hard and it's time to quit, to turn around and go home? I don't know.

I channel Marty's patience and coax Katie up the mountain one treat, one knock-knock joke, one scenic photo stop, one funny story, one hyperbolic compliment at a time. "You're doing it, Katie! You're awesome!" She smiles at my praise, but I cannot say she is having fun.

I start to wonder: whose goal is this anyway?

When Katie comes to a sudden full stop and sits down, we are very near the top. I could run there in five or ten minutes. "No." That is all she says: *no.*

"We're almost there, sweetie. You're going to love it. One more push. It'll be worth it, I promise."

"No. I hate this." She doesn't cry anymore. She sits with her arms folded across her chest and meets my eyes. She's strong and resolute and completely finished.

I sit down where I am. I think of my breathing coach, tuck my knees to my chest, plant my feet on the ground, and let myself be carried.

This is not a race.

There is no finish line.

"You know what I like about this, Katie?"

"What?" She hasn't budged.

"You wouldn't say that to anyone. If you were hiking with another family, you wouldn't say *I hate this*. You wouldn't say *I hate this* to a teacher. Thanks for trusting me enough to tell me how you feel."

She stares at me, suspicious.

"Plus," my voice rings with enthusiasm, "I like your assertiveness, your ability to express yourself forcefully. You don't seem shy at all."

I pull a sweatshirt out of my pack and fluff it up on the ground next to me, pat it, signaling for Katie to come closer and sit on its cushion. She slides next to me, but she's rigid. I put my arm around her sweaty shoulders and say nothing until she's ready. Eventually, I feel her body relax into my side. I kiss the top of her head. "I'm sorry this is so hard, Katie. Thank you for telling me you feel that way. Look where we are, though." The mountains loom around us. A friend once described the "roaring silence" he hears where the mountains meet the sky. "Their phenomenal presence should be deafening," he said, "but there's only imposing quiet."

"Isn't it amazing?!" I put a hand on each of Katie's cheeks and kiss her forehead. "You got here on your own two legs. We might as well finish, don't you think? And then I promise I will take your hatred of hiking into consideration when I make all future plans."

Katie wrinkles her nose and growls at me, a low vibration from her tonsils.

"I'm joking." I run my hand down her torso and rub circles on her back. "Thaumazein," I say pointing at the peaks. "That's the word Greeks used for the way nature inspires a sense of wonder and awe so overwhelming it leads to great thought. Like, the mountains make us want to understand the mysteries of — actually never mind. I'm ruining the idea with words. *Thaumazein*," I say and wave my hand toward the enormous silence of the mountains. We sit and watch. Katie seems content in the stillness. We stay in the quiet for a long, comfortable while. "Look," I finally say. "We can turn back if you want. We really can. We're twenty minutes from the top, though. Do you want to have worked as hard as you have and not make the top?" Is this me proving myself unable to escape the finish-what-you-start, no-pain-no-gain mentality of my upbringing, or do I simply want all her effort to be rewarded by the high of a summit? "Twenty more minutes."

"You always say that."

I look to the peak, do some mental calculations. "I promise this time. Not more than twenty minutes. Maybe even less." Katie does not say no. "You know the main lesson here?"

"Do not come hiking with Mom?"

I'm happy to see her mischievous lopsided smile. "No. Prepare ahead. A while back, I reviewed a running memoir for my book column. Someone decided to do a marathon without training — because there was symbolic significance to finishing the race. So she had to walk a lot and she took the maximum allowed time to finish and she knew she would injure herself, but she finished. I completely understood why she did that, but her doing the race unprepared still annoyed me, as an athlete. The point of sports is in the preparation, the lead up. You and I did not prepare for this hike. We should have gone to bed early. We should have started first thing in the morning, feeling fresh, before the day got hot, before we got tired. That's the lesson: prepare."

"I have a lesson." I hear a laugh emerging in Katie's voice. "Next time, instead, let's go *water-sliding*."

Last weekend, the four of us went to an amusement park, with waterslides, in Idaho. Marty and Katie love theme parks — the crowds, the junk food, the rides. Ollie and I could live happily without ever stepping onto a Tilt-A-Whirl, a roller coaster, a Panic Plunge, or even a Ferris wheel. For years, the visit to Silverwood Theme Park was a father-daughter weekend, a midsummer trip that Ollie and I opted out of. Two years ago, Marty suggested we all go. "I'll set you and Ollie up at the water park. Some towels, a tent, your books. You'll love it."

That's what we do now: we all go. This year, wanting to save money on a hotel, I suggested we drive home to Canada after enjoying a full day of sugar and adrenaline. Since I posed the cost-saving measure, I also offered to drive.

I am a terrible driver.

Just past Bonners Ferry, I pulled out to pass a truck. We'd decided Marty should sleep as long as he could and then take over, but I sensed him awake and tense in the passenger seat. "What?" I tried not to snap, but driving makes me edgy, and I felt uncomfortable behind the wheel of Marty's big truck.

"That guy gave you the finger," Marty said. "You might have been tailgating."

"Really? How much distance should I leave?"

"About a car's length . . . at least two seconds."

"Oh. Whoops. I *was* close then."

"Yep. I didn't want to say anything." Marty leaned his head back toward the window as if he might try to sleep more, but then sat straight up. "And there's um—" He pointed his thumb over his shoulder.

The blue and red of a police lightbar lit up my rearview mirror.

"Mom!" Suddenly, Ollie and Katie came alive in the back seat, yelling over each other, vibrating with stress. They'd never before been pulled over by the police.

"Shhh. Shhh. Settle down. It's okay. It's fine." I spoke into the dark windshield as I rounded a corner, looking for a shoulder safe enough to lead the truck to the side of the road, but I suddenly felt awkward driving this big vehicle. It was too dark and I was tired and I'd just had an irksome thought cross my mind, one that would not improve our situation. "Marty. Don't get mad. But I just realized: I don't have my driver's license. Remember this morning at the park entrance when I couldn't find my Visa? My license is in the same wallet, at home. Don't say anything. Let me talk."

Marty only had time to sigh as he rolled down the window where a flashlight shone in his face.

"Hello, ma'am," the officer said, looking across Marty without acknowledging him. "Do you know how fast you were going?"

"No," I said. "I'm sorry. This truck is in kilometers. We're from Canada. Your signs are all in miles. I get a little confused. And I'm not really used to this truck. I'm sorry," I said again. "How fast was I going?"

"Well, ma'am, if I tell you, I'll have to give you a ticket. That's the law. You also seemed to be having trouble maintaining your lane." He kept his face and voice serious. I often get lucky with

Americans in positions of authority. One time pulling through the border, I drove right into a pylon. The border officer, without a hint of a smile, said, "First I'll ask you what you do for a living. I'm guessing you're not a driving instructor."

I did not get a joker this time, though. "Okay," I said. "Here's what happened. Back there I was tailgating someone. I'm a terrible driver. So my husband was explaining about tailgating, and I guess I was focused on what he was saying instead of focusing on driving well, and I really shouldn't drive. It's his truck. I don't even like driving. But we're just going home from Silverwood, back to Canada, and I wanted to let him rest for a bit. He's probably going to take over now."

"Can I see your driver's license, ma'am?"

"Of course." I pretended to search through my purse, digging out receipts and Kleenex and sunscreen and lipstick and hair elastics and dropping it all in my lap, bills floating to the floor. "You know what? I don't seem to have it. It's in the same wallet as my credit cards. I don't seem to have that either. I must have lost them at the theme park."

"You have no driver's license?"

"No. I think I lost it. I'm not having a very good day."

He instructed us to wait and returned to his car. As soon as he moved out of earshot, the kids exploded again: pure, loud stress. *"Mom, seriously, what?!"*

"You could have given him your passport," Marty said.

"You think? Instead of a license?"

"At least it would prove who you are. Not a convicted criminal."

"Mom, this is really serious, what if —"

Katie watched wide-eyed and silent as Ollie reeled off his alarming list of what-ifs. Marty and I were still trying to calm them down when the flashlight returned to the passenger window. Ollie and Katie fell silent, studying their laps.

"Do you have any ID at all, ma'am?"

"We were talking about that just as you left. My husband said he bet my passport would help! I have a passport!"

"Yes, ma'am. Your passport would certainly help." He took my passport and left again.

Minutes later, his flashlight shone on Marty's face. Marty unrolled the window for a third time. "Ma'am. We have a number of offenses here. I should fine you one hundred dollars for speeding, three hundred and fifty dollars for failure to maintain your lane, five hundred dollars for driving without a license, and . . . well. I am going to pretend I don't even know about the tailgating."

So much for saving money on a hotel room. Marty slumped between us, holding a hand to each side of his head, blocking himself from our exchange. He and the police officer seemed to have some sort of man-pact to not acknowledge each other. Neither of them smiled once. I had the feeling that if one of them cracked and laughed, they'd both dissolve in giggles.

"Switching drivers would be a good idea, ma'am," the officer said, his face devoid of emotion. "I support that decision."

He watched Marty and me climb across each other, changing spots to get Marty behind the wheel. I wanted to wave to him as he continued to stand there on the shoulder of the highway, not moving to return to his car until we'd driven out of sight. In the end, he hadn't issued me a single ticket.

"What was that?!" Ollie burst out as soon as Marty pulled the truck back on the highway.

"Mom Jedi mind tricked him," Katie laughed.

"I did!" I waved my hand in front Ollie's face: *"I'm such a bad driver it's funny."* I lowered my tone to mimic the American police officer: *"You're such a bad driver it's funny."* I waved my hand again: *"You're not even going to give me a ticket."* Wave. *"I'm not even going to give you a ticket."*

Marty shook his head. "I couldn't even look at him. And when he asked for your license? *Driver's license? I don't have a driver's license. Have you seen me drive? Who would give me a driver's license?"* The kids laughed from the back, loving their dad's performance. "I thought what will she say next? Hold up a baggy and ask, *I can't remember, officer: is marijuana even legal here?* I think the guy felt sorry for me." Marty laughed again — "Oh my god, Ang!" — then he faked an awkward juggling motion: *"Oh my! Where should I put this loaded handgun, officer?!"*

Ollie and Katie folded over and laughed into their knees, wiping tears of hilarity from their faces. "We're lucky," Ollie announced when he got his breath, "that we're not in jail!"

I twisted in my seat, enjoying the sight of my children laughing together, getting along the way they used to when they were small.

"I'm a terrible driver," Marty mimicked again in a high, ditzy voice. "I have no idea what just happened. Why *aren't* you in jail?"

All summer, I have been hoping a season of hiking would create memories. I overestimated my powers.

Memories create themselves.

This is the family moment Ollie and Katie will most remember from the summer of 2019: my terrible driving, a dumbfounded American policeman, my Jedi mind trick, and Marty's joke about the baggy of pot. *I can't remember, officer, is marijuana even legal here?*

Driver's license?! Have you seen me drive? Who would give me a driver's license?!

I am right. Katie and I arrive at the mountaintop in slightly over fifteen minutes. Plus, the last ten minutes turn out to be a sporty scramble with high consequence for any missteps. Katie's favorite. The more risk, the more fun. That risk-to-fun ratio, I'm realizing, is a basic truth of Katie World. She attacks the slope on all fours, stretching to get a good hold on the rocks above her. Suddenly, she is all light. By the time we reach the peak, her mood has changed entirely. She is absolutely pleased, with herself, with the mountain, with the day. I love the self-assurance in her smile, the confident set of her shoulders, the intensity of her gaze. The emotional weather continues to improve from here. After some rest and some food, Katie is downright jubilant. She stands on top of the highest rock and looks over the valley. In her small features, I can see the *wow* of it all, the pure splendor of this grand, beautiful, wild world.

I have spent most of the afternoon questioning my motivation. Why push? What is the value of these hikes? Now, to see Katie elated, proud of where she is — on top of the world by virtue of her own power, her own effort, her own endurance — I am glad I pushed.

To promote *Home Ice*, I've been doing speaking tours with famous hockey dad Karl Subban, retired teacher and principal, as well as father to National Hockey League stars P.K., Malcolm, and Jordan. My speeches tend to focus on taking the pressure off children, pushing less in sports, and letting kids be kids. Karl smiles affably and agrees with me sometimes, but he always adds a knowing "I've never met a kid who doesn't need some pushing." Katherine Martinelli, writing for the Child Mind Institute, has advice on when to push children and how to distinguish between helpful encouragement and pushing too hard. She explains that

Dr. Harold S. Koplewicz, a psychiatrist and founding president of the Child Mind Institute, says being able to tolerate discomfort leads to grittiness and resilience. Powering through difficulty teaches kids confidence. To this end, pushing does have its benefits; Dr. Koplewicz, however, stresses the importance of knowing and reading each child to assess limits. He also encourages parents to engage in self-reflection to be sure of the motivation behind our push. What does *the child* want? Are we pursuing *the child's* passions? Is this direction in *the child's* best interest?

In *Psychology Today*, Dr. Stuart Shanker claims previous generations had an easy answer to "when is it good to push?" *It's always good*. Sadly, Dr. Shanker demonstrates that the old approach led to mood changes, anxiety, and a loss of enjoyment of games or activities. He emphasizes, "Perseverance is fueled by interest and desire." Someone else pushing does not create interest or desire. Dr. Shanker separates reasons to persist in a difficult activity into two categories: perseverance versus compulsion. In the latter, driven by expectation of external reward or fear of punishment, children push beyond their body's warnings to potentially detrimental effects, possibly even limbic system crash. Compulsion will eventually be exhausting, whereas perseverance, associated with individual desire and flow state, energizes. Parents must learn to read their child's body language — eyes, voice, posture, movement — and recognize when gentle but firm pushing will not keep those children going in any kind of positive, life-affirming fashion. Ignoring the physical signs of fatigue — and not prioritizing the child's intrinsic motivation, enthusiasm, and desire — will result in children burning out and likely quitting the activity as soon as they become old enough to realize they have that power.

Katie stands on the highest rock, her messy hair whipping around her face. I crawl my way out to her and hand her a jacket. The wind blows cool up here, though she looks unaffected. She's fired up on her accomplishment, no remnants of the anguish that got her here. She appears to have forgotten how much she wanted to go home. I watch her pace the ridge, one careful step at a time, delicately placing each foot, a gymnast on a balance beam. She loses herself in the view for chunks of time, and then checks over her shoulder to make sure I'm there, still watching her.

I am.

When she stops to sit on a rock, I join her. The resting spot is sharp and jagged, but she doesn't complain. We share a bag of cherries, mostly in silence.

She points at the biggest mountain. "Quietly loud," she says softly. She spits a cherry pit into the deep valley at her feet. "Or is it loudly quiet?"

Eventually, I ask her, "Are you happy now? That we didn't turn back?"

She shrugs, playing it cool. "I guess." Then a smile overtakes her, spreading across her face, matching the intense light in her eyes. "It *is* pretty amazing up here."

"It is," I agree. "Good for our souls."

As writer-in-residence at my university, Steven Heighton gave a talk about illusion (published as *The Virtues of Disillusionment*). He spoke of many kinds of illusion, including that of progress or hope — the idea of life as a forward trajectory with the implicit belief that through our goals and effort we eventually arrive at a conclusion, a reward, a payoff. Afterward, he and I discussed ways the day-to-day lives of writers and athletes often hinge upon that illusion, the hope of future success that will make our names and, allegedly, leave us feeling whole and worthy. "Ultimately, though, that linear view of life, with its illusion of arrival, is a death wish," Steven said. "First, because if you're always looking ahead, you're dead to what's alive around you now. Second, because there's only one place we all arrive for sure, and looking ahead hurries you toward it."

The grave.

Steven's essay quotes Lawrence Durrell who, invoking Buddhist notions of the instability or "emptiness" of all concepts, including that of a fixed self, claims that personality itself is an illusion — an illusion upon which romantic, erotic love depends. How can we devote ourselves to someone for life, as we do in marriage vows, if we don't believe in a fixed, stable self? If our erotic partner has no essential self, what is it that we love? Couples therapist Esther Perel, author of *The State of Affairs,* claims she has had three husbands (but all three happen to be the same man). Perhaps a marriage's longevity depends upon this flexibility to adjust to the new (ever-changing) person sharing our bed.

Let's acknowledge that Heighton, Durrell, and Perel likely overstate the extent of personality-as-illusion for effect. While Perel's husband may have changed in dramatic ways over the years, surely he has core characteristics that make him recognizable as the same person. Some child psychologists, like Christopher Nave, indicate that our key personality traits harden into place by first grade: a talkative child will be a talkative adult; adaptable children become cheerful grown-ups; kids who are less impulsive than their peers most likely demonstrate fearfulness in adulthood. Other psychologists, like Dan McAdams, claim personality (as a succinct picture of a person's emotions, behaviors, and attitudes) begins to emerge in a clear and consistent fashion with adolescence.

I try to hold onto both views of personality — that of the philosophers and that of the scientists. Everyone has some core, identifiable personality traits, *and* none of us can count on a fixed whole that we call "personality," neither in ourselves nor in those whom we love. Changes and shifts can be unpredictable. Those transformations will likely challenge marriages, other romantic relationships, and even friendships.

With young children, we know they will change and grow, that they don't yet have fixed personalities. Since we never have that illusion of their personality as stable and unchanging, our love does not depend on it.

What *do* I love about my preteen daughter if she does not yet (and may never) have a fixed, essential self? Partly, my love of her is physical, made up of sensations I feel in my body: the fullness in my chest when I watch her, serene and satisfied on the top of a mountain, or the electric jolt to my gut when I realize how fast she's shedding the skin of childhood. Partly, I love to watch my daughter try on different selves, deciding who she will be.

Over dinner, after Steven's talk, I admitted to being stuck on one point, worrying my way through it. "I think I write memoir in an attempt to drop illusions, trying to see life clearly, free of the scripts and performances, hoping that my honesty will help other people see their lives clearly too."

He nodded, with me so far.

"But then, of course, as memoirists, we massage and shape and shine our lives into coherent and ordered stories. We turn our people into fixed and clear personalities, into characters. We have to engage in this molding to make a book out of the chaos and confusion. But then, aren't we creating an illusion — the ultimate illusion? And . . . isn't it hypocritical to claim to be dropping illusions, while doing so in a form that is itself an illusion?"

Steven took time to think before answering. "No," he finally said, the word a solid stone. I liked his confidence. "The illusion of a book is different because the reader knows."

"It's like a contract . . ."

"Yes, a contract. A book is an illusion the writer and reader agree on, in pursuit of a higher truth."

Katie speeds down the mountain. This time, I try to keep up. Ignoring my knees' protest, I take the slope at a slight jog, right on Katie's heels. With the pressure of the climb behind us, our silences feel natural and relaxed. I do not try to fill them. Gradually, Katie begins to talk, opening each offering with a timid "Mom . . ."

"Mom . . . what do you think I should do for the Blue Lake Camp talent show?"

"Mom . . . what would you buy first with infinite money?"

"Mom . . . if you could live anywhere in the world, where would you live?"

We decide she will dance for the talent show, and that if I had infinite money, I would buy new floors. She finds my choice infinitely dull. I guess I agree, but I tell her by fixing my house, I am buying freedom from aggravation.

"I would buy a house in Victoria!"

"You've never been to Victoria."

"Juan de Fuca is right by Victoria."

"I will visit you there," I tell her.

"Mom . . . what do you think came first, *bug* the action or *bug* the thing? Like, did we say, 'he's bugging me,' and then since insects bug people, we started calling them bugs? Or did we call insects bugs, and then because insects annoy us . . . well you know? Which way?"

"It's easier without the boys, isn't it? For you and me to get a bit of time together to talk."

"Jupiter more stupider," Katie laughs. "Ollie talks a *lot*."

"Well, yes he does. I love his talk, but I love a chance to talk to you too."

At the vehicle, we high five. On impulse, I reach my hand out for our shake. It's been a while, but she meets me with no hesitation.

The next weekend, my sister-in-law visits. In 2004, Lyndsay qualified for Team Canada and competed in the first match of women's wrestling at an Olympic Games. She stays ridiculously fit, and I know she'll be up for whatever outdoor adventure is on offer. I haven't quite let go of the mother-daughter peak-a-week goal, so I urge Katie to come along. "We'll do one from Island Lake Lodge," I say. "That way we can drive high to begin with. The hike won't be as onerous."

Katie drags herself up the trail, and Lyndsay gets a good laugh at the discrepancy between the *ideal* of the peak-a-week challenge and its *reality*.

"We're almost there," I tell Katie.

"You've been saying that," Katie scowls, "for *three hours*."

Lyndsay laughs. "Katie, she can't have been saying it for three hours. We've only been hiking for ninety minutes."

"Oh, Lyndz," I admit. "I have been saying 'we're almost there' for dozens of hours, for weeks. I've been saying 'we're almost there' all summer."

The fun has gone out of Katie's run, as we used to say in marathon training. She only shows enthusiasm briefly when we pass through a boulder-filled section and I let her veer off the trail to climb the big rocks. Hiking itself doesn't interest her. It's not that hiking is too hard, I realize, but that it's too dull. She needs an activity that offers an adrenaline rush to offset the effort. In the terms of Dr. Stuart Shanker, we have shifted from perseverance (associated with internal desire, flow state, enthusiasm) to compulsion (associated with pushing, bribing, and punishing, even if only in the form of verbal criticism or perceived disappointment), and we need to shift tracks before my daughter experiences a limbic crash.

Back on the trail, we pass a man a bit older than me. He walks with trekking poles, going slowly with a serene smile on his face. "Isn't it just gorgeous," I say as we pass.

"Absolutely," he beams. "I love it. I try to get here a few times a year, at least."

"My daughter's not enjoying it. I'll tell you that." I point my thumb over my shoulder where Katie lags, her face a pout.

"Well," he says. "I coached track for years. I know kids. Parents have to remember, kids have small legs. Hiking is harder for kids."

This man's advice reminds me of my university swim coach. One morning he pulled me out of practice. "You don't want to be here," he said. "You never miss practice. I know. But you can. There's no sense swimming if you don't want to. Get out." He said it kindly. He did not tell me to leave as a reprimand, but as a life lesson. My self-worth should not be intrinsically bound to a stubborn adherence to goals.

We're almost there, look how far we've come, just another hour, just another twenty minutes, just around the next corner. I see the relentless push of our summer hikes — relentlessly linear, relentlessly focused on arrival, relentlessly goal-oriented. I seem not to be able to let relentless go.

This summer originated as a step away from organized sport. After writing *Home Ice*, I saw our family's excessive dedication to youth sports and the way athletic commitments divided us. We vowed to make a change, to rethink where we allocated our family's money, energy, and time. Many experts support this step away from elite youth sports. Tom Farrey, in a 2019 *New York Times* article, argues that Norway has found the answer to excess in youth sport. He explains that ninety-three percent of children in Norway grow up playing organized sport, but with no traveling teams or tiering until the teen years. As adults, the nation's athletes are extremely successful. The idea is to give kids a chance to grow into their bodies and unearth their own interests, rather than having parents' interests foisted upon them. If we make sport too intense too early, kids burn out and drop out. Simply, athletic life should focus on the motivation of the child.

I intended this nature immersion as a move away from organized sports, but the track coach appearing midtrail makes me realize that I have brought the mindset of organized sports with us.

In the middle of August, at nearly the end of our peak-a-week summer, I prepare only one backpack. "Katie," I say, "I'm going to go back to Island Lake Lodge and do another hike, not the one we did with Auntie Lyndsay, but similar."

She nods, wary.

"I'm going to go by myself. When I'm back, I'll grab you and we can go to the lake or cliff jumping or . . . whatever you want."

"But . . ." She furrows her brow. "What about Smoke and Fire? What about my goal?"

Her goal. I remember the 2016 study from the *Journal of Neuroscience* about girls learning how to process their emotions from their mothers.

"Well goals are good ideas as long as they're still fun. Once you're doing something you truly don't enjoy, it's time to re-evaluate the goal. I think you've had enough big hikes for the summer, don't you?"

She's still for a moment and then moves her head in the tiniest nod.

"I can think of so many great moments on our hikes this summer. The slug jokes, the Groot leaves, cherries on a mountain peak, the way you race downhill, leaving your poor, slow mom in your dust."

"And climbing on the boulders last week," she adds. "That was really fun. And that scary part at the top of Mount Fernie and getting up on the big rocks by the ocean."

"And I loved all the hours talking to you."

"Yeah, I liked that too."

"See? It's been good, really good. Besides, maybe the peak-a-week part has always been mostly my goal. If I look at what's behind the goal, what's the reason . . . well it's always been about you and I spending more time together, getting outside and enjoying nature. That's the important part: me, you, and the wild. We can accomplish *that* goal other ways."

"I guess . . ."

"You know what I've learned? And it's taken me fifty years, so I'm giving you a shortcut. The end of *anything* always feels a bit sad, even when letting go is the right thing to do. Let's see how you're doing later today."

"Katie!" Marty yells from the mudroom, where I suspect he's been eavesdropping. "Do you have a helmet?"

Katie lights up. "Yes!" She loves activities that involve a helmet. I have a photograph of her as a two-year-old. She'd made a tower of coffee tables and play chairs and sat at the top, wearing pyjamas; a giant, proud smile; and her pink ski helmet. "Safety first," Marty said when I showed him the picture that day after work.

"Should I be relieved that she thought far enough ahead to go get her helmet?"

"I've been checking out Frank Slide in the Crowsnest Pass," Marty says now. "We're allowed to go bouldering there . . . I've been wanting to try it, but I need a buddy. Someone who loves climbing . . ."

"Me!" Katie leaps off her chair, holding her hand in the air. "I do! I love climbing!"

Their smiles match. I feel the love in my body — a warming in my skin, a lifting in my chest, a lightness in my limbs. "*This* excitement," I tell Katie, "this love, this grin —" I tap the corner of her mouth. "*That's* how you *should* feel about the weekend."

I kiss them both goodbye, tell them to be safe, and I go alone.

Eight

What I Talk about When I Talk about Hiking by Myself

Solo hiking is a revelation. I don't need anyone to lead me, or even accompany me, into the beautiful wilderness. I don't need to recruit friends. I don't need to dance around other people's schedules. I don't need to cancel an outing because the weather doesn't meet someone else's expectations. I no longer fret that the grade or location or scenery of a certain hike might not suit a potential companion's preference. If I want to go hiking, I go hiking. Easy. Being able to go alone transforms my life. I spend more time exactly where I want to be: with the trees.

Marty still makes fun of my decisions. One time I take his ultralight backpack from the garage and then stuff it full of bagels, an entire container of cream cheese, heavy kitchen utensils, and (on an especially grand impulse) an icepack.

"Are you serious?" he asks me, fetching his gear scale. The backpack weighs 1.2 pounds; the icepack and butter knife combined come out at 1.5. More than the whole pack. "*Ultralight*, Ang. I think you missed the point. An *icepack?*"

"I like my cheese cool," I tell him. I don't claim to be an outdoors expert. I'm simply doing what I like.

Another time, on possibly the hottest day of summer, I take no sunscreen, no hat, and only one peach. I make the solitary piece of fruit last, forcing myself to wait until the top to eat the first half, then taking nibbles on the way down. I get home hungry, but happy. Marty laughs at each amateur display. Enjoying his good humor, I tell him about getting lost at the start of one hike and circling the first kilometer of trail four times before finding a way forward.

"Are you sure you should even be out there by yourself?"

Yep, I am sure. These small, laughable faux pas aside, I am pleased to discover that I'm quite happy (and competent enough) alone in the wilderness.

Without Katie, I tackle hikes that are bigger, higher, longer, and more remote. I am delighted to find myself up to the task. I start to wonder if proving my competence and comfort on the trails was always an underlying motivation for this hiking plan. I have a long-standing habit of making myself the punchline of every joke, and over the years, my experiences in nature have supplied much material. The first summer after Marty and I married, he landed work at a fire tower on top of an inaccessible mountain. He lived there alone for three months. Near the end of the summer, his employer arranged a "conjugal visit." I was to drive the backcountry roads to a predetermined meeting spot where a helicopter would land and float me up to Marty's shack, with enough supplies to keep him there for another couple of weeks.

I do not like driving steep mountain roads, and I have a poor sense of direction. Fear makes me drive slowly. Experience convinces me I am most likely lost. For the conjugal visit, I worked myself into a state. The trip took me three times as long as Marty told me it should, and I felt sure I'd missed my helicopter. Plus, I thought I'd probably ended up in the wrong spot so the pilot would never find me anyway. When I spotted two men fly-fishing at a river below me, I steered toward them in Marty's 1986 AMC Eagle, nicknamed "Eddy" after Britain's infamous Olympic ski-jumper.

Dressed exactly like a young woman visiting her new husband in a remote fire tower, all short-shorts and bared midriff and big hair, I jumped out of the car and ran for the men. My words spilled into each other in an incomprehensible blur. At race pace, I explained about trying to find a tower where my husband lived on top of a mountain and I couldn't drive all the way up there but a pilot should be meeting me at the bottom of the closest mountain and . . . except maybe I was lost and had they seen any helicopters flying around . . . or maybe I'd missed the pilot entirely because I'd fallen a bit behind schedule trying to navigate this stupid treacherous road and why couldn't mountain roads be less mount—

Just as I really began to gain momentum, I spotted a helicopter. "Wave it down," I told them. "I think it's my ride!"

The three of us waved frantically. When the helicopter veered our direction, I got a sinking, ill feeling. What if this wasn't my helicopter? What if the pilot had taken our intense waving as evidence of an emergency? What if we'd lured these professionals off course when they should be attending to actual emergencies, like the forest fires raging in every direction? As the helicopter got closer, I saw inside its cab, which was stuffed full with firefighters. "Oh no! I don't think it's my helicopter," I said to the strange men, as the heat of humiliation flooded my body. "Stop waving! No! No! Wave it off!"

Despite my no no no and my rapid hand gestures shooing the pilot away and despite the two confused men mimicking my actions, the helicopter got close, growing so loud we couldn't talk. As the three of us backed up to watch it land, I realized the fishermen had not yet spoken to me. I hadn't given them any opportunity.

When the machine made contact with ground, I saw all the firefighters clearly — five of them, faces caked in soot. They jumped out one at a time. The shortest removed a helmet and luscious black hair fell around her shoulders. She smiled wide, her teeth sharp white in contrast to the ash coating her cheeks and chin and forehead.

"Jen?" I recognized her, a gorgeous lifeguard from our local swimming pool. "You're a firefighter?"

"Angie! You're in the totally wrong spot, and you're late, but I recognized Marty's car — Eddy the Eagle! Jump in."

Blushing, I loaded groceries, water, and — to the pilot's dismay — a golden retriever into the cab of the helicopter. The firefighters sat down on a log to wait with the fishermen as the pilot flew me up to join my husband. From the air, I waved goodbye to the two bewildered men who, until fifteen minutes ago, had been enjoying the serenity and solitude of a remote river.

When confronted with these kinds of challenges in the back-country, I have almost always, and for decades, played the roles of dumb blonde and damsel in distress. The performance comes so easily it feels almost natural.

I have excelled at this helpless-woman-lost-in-nature role in both summer and winter. In 2014, two journalists from the *New York Times* visited Fernie to write a story on "British Columbia's Powder Highway." The head honcho in public relations at Resorts of the Canadian Rockies asked me to go out with the New Yorkers and tour them around the ski hill. "You're all writers! You'll hit it off great."

Though appreciative of the potential connection, I felt some skepticism: these two men had come to the Powder Highway to ski steep terrain and deep snow. I suspected they wanted high adrenaline and big adventure. An article about skiing in Fernie should capture the "extreme" culture, of which I am not a part. I felt sure the journalists would have preferred spending a day on the mountain with Marty, not with a middle-aged, bookish woman, who, when it came to skiing, always chose control over speed.

But: the *New York Times*!

I called my friend Amanda, far radder than I am, and begged her to join the three of us. "These guys will want to know things," I told her. "About the mountain. And what do I know? You can tell them!"

On the chairlift, the journalists showed polite interest in my ski-town satire, a novel called *The Canterbury Trail*. Then they asked questions about our little town, about what people do for work, about how often locals ski, about what we think of the tourism boom, about whether Fernie lives up to its reputation as Powder Valley, home of the best snow. So far so good. Then, before we'd even skied our first run, one of them posed a question beyond my abilities. From our seat on the Bear Chair, the journalist pointed toward the top of the mountain, at the Lizard Range, and asked, "Which direction is this?"

I waited for Amanda to answer. She said nothing. I poked her in the side with my elbow. Still nothing. Finally, I had to fill the silence. "Up," I said, with great confidence. "Yeah, typically the ski-lift takes us in what we call the *up* direction, and then we get off, and we ski in the *down* direction."

Over the years, telling and retelling stories like these, I have made myself into a caricature. Bookish but incompetent. "She's *school* smart," my brother likes to say.

Am I as inept as these stories make me out to be? I know that I'm not dumb, or lacking in practical skills, but perhaps I am a little lazy. If I can leave the planning (and the orienteering) to my man, I will.

Alone, I have no choice. I must figure out this world on my own: the gear, the directions, the schedule, the route, the food, the weather, the first aid kit, all of it. The hikes with Katie — and now these hikes by myself — force me into self-sufficiency. Likely, my quest for competency has to do with recently turning fifty, well past the age I should have stopped playing the role of laughable, helpless girl.

To mark my fiftieth, I celebrated by traveling to New York with my two oldest friends, Robyn and Robin. Robyn, Robin, and I have been friends since we were five years old, but New York marked the first time the three of us traveled together. As we trekked around the city, I wondered why I chose to expose Katie to remote places to build her confidence and to focus on our mother-daughter bonding. Why not expose Katie to cityscapes instead?

The city would, in fact, be more foreign to Katie than the forest. An urban center would have provided more of an adventure for a small-town mountain girl too.

In *Wild*, Cheryl Strayed claims "the wilderness had a clarity that included me." I know this feeling. I want Katie to know it too. Clarity is, in fact, the perfect gift for a mother to pass to her daughter in this loud, crazy, complex, and confusing world.

In hiking, I chase the euphoric release that I experienced with the cottonwood tree, the way I floated above the trivial stresses threatening to drown me, how clearly I recognized their insignificance. In my summer's commitment to regular, long nature walks, I have also developed a practice of drawing on the wilderness for the kind of relief that running with Blue in the woods gave me, especially the relief the wild provided from social media–inspired conflicts. I know what I hope to find in nature, what I *do* find there: serenity, strength, resilience, peace. I want to share those feelings with my daughter. I want her to know nature as a place where she can always retreat when she needs to find solace, clarity, and meaning.

Between coming and going from my solitary spells on the mountain, I spend more time with Katie than ever. In wanting to share great experiences, I had forgotten that my perfect day might not be Katie's perfect day. Now, having abandoned the mother-daughter peak-a-week plan and rejigging it as my own goal, I focus our time together on listening and being receptive. I follow Katie's lead as she discovers what a perfect Katie-Day might look like.

After a day bouldering with her dad at Frank Slide, she comes home euphoric.

"She kept looking over her shoulder at me," Marty says, "and asking, 'Are you having *so much fun*, Dad?!'" He laughs. "Over and over again. 'Are you having *so much fun?*' It was adorable. Her smile. 'Yes, Pumpkin,' I said, 'are *you* having so much fun?' She *absolutely* loved it."

As I give Katie space to unfurl, she also shows interest in activities at the other end of the adrenaline spectrum, activities that can include her feet-on-solid-ground mom. Katie develops an intense passion for baking, delving into increasingly complicated recipes and more elaborate decorations. Her specialty of sugar-saturated cake pops salvages her relationship with her brother.

"Um, hey, Katie," Ollie will call sweetly. "Were you maybe thinking of doing some baking today?"

Once, when my writing group visits our house, we notice a little redhead girl park herself around the corner from us, where she can spend the evening eavesdropping. Afterward, Katie confides in me that *she* would like to write a book. The next afternoon, Katie and I take our journals down to the creek, along with a picnic. We have a mother-daughter writing date. Katie sits on a big grey rock in the middle of the creek, white water parting around her, one knee pulled toward her chest, while the other leg dangles, toes in the liquid chill, a journal spread open on her thigh.

We don't always have to engage with nature *athletically*, I realize. On this afternoon, I see Katie enacting thaumazein — using the beauty of nature to inspire thought. She writes silently for more than an hour as bad weather gradually approaches. Dark black clouds hover dramatically, looming low behind Katie's shoulders, but she keeps her pencil moving across her page. I watch for a sign of her letting up, but I see none. When I feel the first raindrops, I fold my chair, collect our Tupperware containers of cheese and fruit, pack our bag, and tell her it's time to go.

"In a minute, Mom," she answers without looking up from her rain-splattered page. "We can go soon. I just need to finish this chapter."

We get home with our teeth chattering and our wet clothes sticking to our skin. "You don't know enough to come in out of the storm?" Marty asks.

"Katie wanted to finish her chapter first." I smile.

"Wow. You two are tough."

"Well. One of us is."

Gradually, Katie gets braver socially. When my writing group comes over, she joins us at the kitchen island, listening to our book talk. My friends, accustomed to Katie's timidity and her tendency to scurry off if anyone so much as looks in her direction, express surprise at her presence. They work to draw her into conversation. Still, Katie stays. She directs her replies to me, rather than to whichever friend asks, but she does answer, speaking clearly and with tremulous, budding confidence.

Soon, Katie begins contributing to our conversation without needing the prodding of my friends' questions. "Mom . . ." she will say, pulling on my sleeve, and then sharing what's on her mind about books and writing, or telling a story about a recent outing with her dad or a baking adventure at home. She will hold my eyes firmly as she talks, as if I am her audience of one, but she speaks loud enough for everyone to hear.

At the writing group's last meeting for the summer, Katie sits in our circle and listens as we go around and share our work-in-progress. When we finish, she slides close to me and tugs my sleeve. "Mom . . ."

Of her own accord, with hardly a tremor, Katie volunteers to read us one of her own stories.

My friends get a small glimpse of the Katie I know.

As Katie sheds her fear, I encounter a new one. I have never before felt afraid at the start of a hike. But as I set off on my biggest solo hike of the summer, my biggest solo hike of *ever*, the hyperactive butterflies of anxiety throw a party in my chest. This walk will take ten to twelve hours, with a vertical elevation of twelve hundred meters over two mountain passes. By the end of the day, I will have covered approximately twenty-two kilometers through bear country with no cell service.

I am simultaneously, and in equal measure, excited and scared.

I quickly recognize both emotions as inappropriate for a long, solo hike. These feelings are too big and too loud, not sustainable as the kilometers wear on with their honeyed birdsong and enchanting sunlight and tender breeze and quiet trees. After the first anxious fifteen minutes, I settle into the day and see this time of wilderness walking for what it is, can, and will be.

The one thing that most defines my day alone?

Calmness.

A writing teacher once advised me to be a terrible god to my characters. Disasters propel story. Bad luck creates plot. When something goes wrong, tension spikes, hooking reader interest. When nothing happens, we have no story.

I like story. I am drawn to its compelling momentum, its exciting twists and turns. Neuroscientists have long explored the ways in which humans come hardwired for story, the ways our survival and happiness depend on it, the way character-driven stories teach empathy and release oxytocin. More recently, scientists have turned their attention to the ways our craving drama can lead to more detrimental effects like social media addiction and online mobbing, particularly when our oxytocin response is triggered by a sense of belonging fueled by exclusion and hatred.

In a world where we can dip into drama as easily as reaching for our phones, learning to step out of narrative — and the kind of conflict that drives it — takes some work.

I realize that solo hiking will teach me to be comfortable — even happy — with nothing at all happening. I will learn to crave that nothingness.

The first part of the hike follows the same route Katie and I took when she announced she hated hiking, but instead of going up and coming right back down, I will go up and over and then down and up another mountain pass, eventually ending at a backcountry lodge where Marty will retrieve me. I wonder if I will find the uphill less onerous and the exposed parts less terrifying when I am not seeing them through concern for my ten-year-old girl.

I do not.

The uphill is a true grunt. An hour in, I catch up to a man dressed in running gear: short-shorts, ankle socks, neon trail shoes, a polypro tank top, and a brimmed mesh hat. He has a belted fanny pack instead of a traditional hiking backpack and a bottle of some neon energy drink strapped to each of his hips. Instead of jogging up the mountain, as he clearly intended, he bends at an awkward angle, taking long walking strides and placing a hand on his knee for support with every step.

"God, this trail," he huffs when I walk up alongside him. He looks about thirty, slight and lean with long sinewy muscles. "Has nobody in this town ever heard of a switchback? The damn thing goes straight up."

"Yep." I smile. "It's a steep one." I resist the urge to tell him about my girl.

"Mountain goats. That's what this trail is fit for. I was going to run, and then I settled on a brisk walk, and now —" he looks to the ground, breathing heavily, with a hand on each knee. "Well, now, I'm doing *this*."

"The view's worth it, though. Keep it up!"

He pulls a bottle of bright pink liquid from his hip holster and cheers me with it as he lets himself fall to the ground and rest.

I go another hour and half before I see anyone else. This time I meet a man older than me, maybe approaching sixty. He wears a big hiking hat with a strap pulled tight under his chin, and he descends the steep slope gingerly, resting weight on a long wooden walking stick before taking each step.

"Beautiful day," I call out as I climb toward him.

"Beautiful day," he echoes, his voice deep and serious. He doesn't smile.

"Make it to the top?"

"Nearly," he says. "About three-quarters. After that, it gets treacherous. I didn't want to risk it. But definitely go that far — well worth the strain."

I nod politely as we pass.

I am surprised to discover the trail does not seem easier at all without Katie. It turns out I wasn't simply being a fearful mother: death at the top is a real possibility. I scare myself a few times by misplacing a foot in zones where falling is definitely not an option.

I feel Katie with me the whole way — *she hated this part; she loved it here; I can't believe I let her hike this section; what a girl!*

I have always had a deep fondness for this hike. It hasn't occurred to me that the new part — where, instead of turning to descend after reaching the top, I carry on to explore the terrain behind the mountain — will bring new delights. But when I drop over the ridge onto the backside of the mountain, away from the town and the highway below, the complete absence of noise pollution strikes me.

The intensity of the deep silence combined with the infinite expansiveness of nature so move me that I nearly cry. I remember a friend's explanation of Buddhist tears, and I recognize my swell of emotion as a symptom of my realization of the enormity of this beauty arriving simultaneously with an understanding of my own time here as fleeting.

I have the great fortune to experience the grandness of it all, but only for a moment. I am very small.

Gradually, as I move away from the section I have hiked with Katie, my thoughts drift from my daughter. Alone, I am more aware of the intimate relationship I can have with nature itself. When I smell the cedar trees, that act is the only thing I am doing: smelling the cedar trees. I don't interrupt the sensation by constantly vocalizing my response.

"Isn't it beautiful, Katie?!"

"Smell that air — so fresh!"

"Doesn't the breeze feel great on your skin?"

"Do you love it? I love it!"

Without words, I sink into the experience. I delight in the feeling of wind drying my sweat after the uphill effort. I let myself be overwhelmed by the beauty of the forest and the mountains. I don't pull out my camera each time I see an eagle. I stop. I stand. I watch. Hiking by myself introduces me to a world outside of words and story, a space beyond story's dependence on conflict, its relentless appetite for tension and drama, its notions of good protagonists and evil antagonists. The mountains don't care about any of it. I find their indifference calming.

In an article in *Psychology Today*, developmental psychologist Marilyn Price-Mitchell argues that to be happy, humans need to find meaning in life, and meaning comes through self-reflection, and self-reflection only comes in silence. With today's constant noise of social media, we must work harder than ever to find silence. Too often, we shift our focus from the pleasure of doing something to the pleasure of telling everyone we did it. Performing happiness in our various social media streams, we forget we can quietly sit for a moment in that happiness, rest there, reflect. In these final days of summer, I teach myself to enjoy the experience of nature in a new way, a way that allows me a wonderful reprieve from the spoken and written word.

We need silence to find out what we think. We need silence to rest the mind and regenerate brain cells, reduce stress hormones, lower blood pressure, and improve the immune system. We need silence to listen to what the world has to say to us.

I do have moments alone on the mountain when I am afraid. I see fresh cougar scat and remember what I know of cougars: *If you see one, it's too late. A cougar will rip out your throat.* "A cougar," Marty told me, "will bite down on your head, clutching your

183

temples in its jaws so you can't escape, while it disembowels you with its powerful hind legs and razor sharp claws." He pronounced "powerful" and "razor sharp" with energetic admiration, as if commentating a sporting event. *Thanks, Marty.* Each time I hear rustling in the trees or the bullet crack of a broken twig, I imagine what would happen if I encounter a cougar — or a grizzly — out here alone, a half-day hike from anywhere.

Each time, I talk myself down. What's the worst that could happen? Well, I could die, quite painfully and in terror. But what's the likelihood? I have lived in the mountains for over twenty years, and nobody in the area has been killed by a bear or a cougar. I have more reason to fear getting in a car, which I do every day. Do I want to let fear of wild animals rob me of this experience?

No, I do not.

When Marty and I met on the university swim team in Ontario, he was a young twenty-two-year-old living in a cheap, dirty apartment with four guys, and I was a married twenty-six-year-old with a mortgage, almost three university degrees, and a defined career path. At the end of that year, Marty finished his undergraduate degree and went surfing in Southeast Asia with a girlfriend. Eventually, he found himself single and living in a ski town, enjoying the powder, the party lifestyle, and the masculine camaraderie, but missing female companionship. After the bars closed, oblivious to time zones and craving a female voice in the dark, Marty often called me, where I lived on the other side of the country. I loved Marty, so it only took one ring for me to slip from under the down duvet I shared with my husband. I always answered, no matter how late.

Over the next two years, I worked my way out of that first marriage, moving into a sad bachelor suite in someone's basement. In this reduced circumstance, it was often *I* who called Marty in *my* lonely moments.

During that year of upheaval, Marty gave me one bit of advice that has stayed with me. "Ang," he said, "you have to make yourself strong."

I suspect that's what a twenty-five-year-old man says to a twenty-nine-year-old woman when he feels partially responsible for her divorce, for her life disintegrating before transforming into something new. Even then, I understood the "get strong" line as Marty's way of relieving himself of responsibility. *Don't look to me, lady: you make yourself strong.*

Nonetheless, I knew him to be right. "Yes," I thought as soon as I heard his words, "that's it exactly: I have to make myself strong. But how? What do I do?"

I doubt Marty has any memory of this conversation. We have never over our many years together spoken of his advice. But I have carried those words with me everywhere. *I have to make myself strong.* I played the sentence over in my mind, fidgeting with it like a worry stone deep in my pocket, for two and a half decades.

On the backside of that mountain, on my longest solo hike, I release my lingering confusion and doubt. As I divert my path around fresh cougar scat, as I hear animal noises in the woods and swallow my terror, as I step up and down mountain trails, hours past exhaustion, my uncertainty dries up and evaporates. Life is one long solo hike. By the end of summer, with the help of the mountain and the trees, I no longer need to dwell on young Marty's advice. I have finally done it. I have finally made myself strong.

Nine

In Praise of Boring

My backcountry confidence has reached an all-time high when Jowita Bydlowska, author of the best-selling memoir *Drunk Mom*, comes to visit. "Take me hiking," she says. "We can do all kinds of crazy outdoor stuff. People think I'm big city, but I'm Polish. I'm good with nature. We Eastern Europeans do all that intense wilderness stuff. I know how to make my own bed in the forest, out of fallen branches."

I can't think of a single thing to say. A mutual friend describes Jowita as a woman genetically engineered to dance all night on speakers blasting techno. *She can make a bed? Out of fallen branches?*

"I'm hard-core," she adds, with a hint of jest. She flexes, and a healthy bicep pops on her deceptively skinny arm. "Take me to the adventure!"

Jowita is right. I *do* think she's big city. Everything about this gorgeous woman denotes urban glamor: her lipstick, her waif figure, her cigarettes. "Okay," I tell her. "We'll go for a hike. Be warned, though. I'm writing a hiking book. If you come on the trail with me, you might be in the book."

"Nope," she responds. "I will be as boring as fuck."

"Spoken as a true memoir writer. You know the only sure way out of any book: be dull!"

I cannot imagine Jowita Bydlowska being boring as fuck. She's like a female lead from a James Bond movie: alluring Polish accent, long legs, tight clothes, dramatic sex life. Here in Fernie, Jowita will not blend. I imagine local doctors' offices flooded with cases of whiplash, but I do expect our *hikes*, at least, to be noneventful.

We start out that way, pleasantly dull. Jowita and I complete two vigorous half-day hikes early in the week. Having led city friends into trouble in the past, I proceed with caution. Within the first kilometer of hike number one, we find a closed-trail sign. A mama moose and her calf have been hanging out in the area. *Aggressive*, the sign warns. *Extreme danger!*

Well behaved, Jowita and I backtrack and pick another trail. "Tough call," I tell her. "I am not worried about getting hurt, not as long as we give the animals a wide berth. I'm more concerned about getting scolded by the trail crew." I also suspect that my getting this fancy city woman in backcountry trouble would be delightful news for the small-town gossips. I aim to avoid the potential humiliation.

Jowita doesn't mind our detour. She's happy to walk around the scenic lake below the lodge, taking photographs of the mountains reflected in the green water. I, however, have summits on my mind this summer, and I steer us to a different trail that leads to a mountaintop. Jowita steps in front, and I walk behind, snapping pictures of a beautiful woman in a beautiful place. In the valley below us, the forest, lush and green, glistens with life. Other years, by now, the larch have changed colors, needles falling to the ground. The shock of gold covering the trails in late August always comes as a surprising knell, marking the end of summer, though Marty has told me that the larch turn early not because of a temperature drop marking the transition to autumn, but because of drought-induced stress. This year has been the wettest summer in recent years. We've avoided serious threat of fires, and the larch continue to thrive into the season's final days.

"You must find it easier than I do to not drink," Jowita says, gesturing her hand over the miles and miles of vibrant forest below us. Jowita, like so many people, views her own non-drinking as a lifelong work-in-progress. "Walking is good for addiction, and walking here, well . . ."

She trails off, but I don't need her to finish. She's right: when I need relief from stress, I can turn to this natural beauty instead of to the bottle, and I've been doing so more and more, going months without a drink. My tendency toward excess does not serve me well when it comes to alcohol. "Let's go for a glass of wine" always — *always!* — turns into more than one. A bottle of wine might kill my stress and calm my nerves, but I wake up the next morning feeling dirty on the inside, my limbs heavy with poison, skin grimy, tongue thick and dry, my mind dulled with self-loathing. *You overdid it again, dumdum.* Being out here distracts me from stress at least as effectively as drinking does, and I wake up the next day feeling cleansed, energized for more outdoor adventure. "I read that walking helps battle substance abuse by increasing dopamine," I tell Jowita, "especially a strenuous uphill or brisk walk. If we get that dopamine hit regularly through hiking, we don't crave drugs or alcohol to trigger the high."

A 2018 study in *The Scandinavian Journal of Public Health* determined that when people who overdrink participate in a vigorous exercise program twice a week for as little as thirty minutes each time, they decrease their drinking by eighty-one percent in only one month.

"But it's not just the exercise," I say after a few minutes of walking in silence. "*Nature* helps me not crave alcohol too . . . the way I feel out here, part of something bigger than myself, spiritually, I mean."

"Sure." Jowita says to the trail ahead of her. It's so quiet we don't need to turn and address our comments to each other. There's nobody in the world but us. "Anything that gives pleasure can distract you from addiction. As long as you don't get addicted to the new pleasure!"

When we reach a long stretch of big boulders, I focus on my footing as I climb, and I drop the talk of addiction. Since the publication of Jowita's *Drunk Mom*, over drinkers from around the world treat Jowita like a free therapist, her inbox always bloated with dramatic tales of alcohol abuse. Jowita has collected more than enough drinking stories. She doesn't need mine, not today. "Would you ever do it again?" I ask. "Write a memoir?"

She makes a bemused noise in the back of her throat, neither a yes nor a no. I know what she means. Why would *any* sane person expose herself and her people in the way required by memoir? It's not worth it. Who needs the drama or the judgment? Why do we do it? Her answer should be *No, absolutely not,* but she's a writer, compelled by definition to turn the mess of life into well-shaped paragraphs, publishable pages. Yes, she might write a memoir again, if she can't help it.

"Well," she finally answers, "my ex and I have a deal: if I do write one, I can only put him in it if I give him a huge penis."

We laugh long and easy. Though we both struggle with depression at times, on these rigorous hikes together, we're quite joyful. The magnificent summits, rambling forests, and serrated peaks impress Jowita, exactly as I expect them to excite someone from Toronto. Lean and full of energy, she has no trouble at all with the physical challenge (though we never get the opportunity for her to prove her claim about a forest-made bed). We spend glorious, hot summer days immersed in wonder. Our time together is perfect. Then, on her last day in the Canadian Rocky Mountains, Jowita says, "Let's do something *big*."

I do not hesitate. "Yes," I agree. "Let's do it! Something *big*."

The two of us, our manic energy, our minimal experience, our gleeful decision to "go big" — *what could possibly go wrong?* I almost say it aloud, but already my mind has turned to selecting a truly grand adventure, a spectacular send-off fitting for Jowita Bydlowska's last day in the Rockies.

Over the summer, I've become more comfortable driving mountain roads. I can hold a speed of sixty kilometers per hour, a dust cloud roaring up around me. I hug the safe side of the road, the one without a cliff drop, and never let myself look to the cavernous fall on the other side. *Look where you want to go.* That's what I learned from mountain biking. If you look to the danger, you end up in the danger. The advice works for driving too. For most activities in life. *Look where you want to go.*

The road to the trailhead scares Jowita. She clenches the door handle, her complexion wan. I lighten my foot on the gas pedal and steer even closer to the mountain side of the road, where a slip would have us heading only into a ditch or the cut bank rather than rolling to a flaming death. I remember this fear well and do what I can to alleviate it. The reassuring gap I create between our vehicle and the steep fall loosens Jowita's tongue, but when she begins to talk, she expresses mostly reservations.

"I don't know — maybe we should do something else today. I'm not sure . . ."

She tells me about a conversation with a new boyfriend who told her dark stories of this mountain's history, and then about a dream of mountain mishap. Her stories hang in the truck cab, faintly ominous. I can't believe she wants to back out now. We're here, ready to go, and the weather could not be more perfect. I love the heat. I've been waiting all summer for a scorcher like today.

I make light of her nerves. "You'll love it!" I bounce in my seat, giddy about the day ahead — about showing my friend my stunning home, demonstrating my backcountry prowess, veering from the more tourist-friendly terrain marked by easy-to-follow trail maps, guiding Jowita through a brand-new experience, doing "something *big*." I will not let a bad dream or a gloomy boyfriend spoil our final day together.

Color returns to Jowita's cheeks as we start stepping our way up the mountain. We've been walking maybe forty-five minutes when two big huskies gallop up the trail behind us, rubbing fur against our bare calves as they pass. Two women — a little younger than Jowita, a lot younger than me — come speed walking toward us, shortly after their dogs. The women say brief greetings and then walk right past us as if we're barely moving. Huh. We pick up the pace, our egos a little tender, watching the women and their dogs disappear up the trail.

Jowita and I don't talk about getting passed so easily, but we quit pausing for pictures and walk quickly enough that we both break into a sweat.

Thirty more minutes into our brisk hike, the path ends. It just stops. Jowita and I don't stop, though. We follow a wet curve in the ground and duck under the large trunk of a fallen tree. We follow the groove of wet mud upward. It's kind of a trail, I rationalize. It's trail-like. A mudslide or a water drainage has created a natural line through the foliage; we follow that. Within minutes, the grade of our ascent switches from a hike to a climb, the kind of climb that requires all four limbs.

"This can't be it," I yell up at Jowita. "Katie would love this — the scramble, the adrenaline. The danger. But I've done this hike with Katie, and she most definitely did *not* love it, not at all. I would remember this terrain. It can't be right."

Jowita nods and follows me back down to where we initially lost the trail. We stand there again, stumped. There's nowhere else to go. I don't remember this dead end from my earlier adventure with Katie, yet here it is. Either we turn back, or we duck under the fallen tree and climb up the crevice. "But those two women," Jowita says. "They didn't come back. They must've gone *somewhere*." Jowita looks antsy, keen to keep walking. I too feel jacked up on adrenaline.

"You're right. It must be this way," I say, even though I know it's not. "Let's go." We duck back under the toppled tree and climb up the damp path.

At first, I love the climb. I understand Katie's draw to scary terrain. "This is fun," I yell up to Jowita as I stretch an arm high above me to get a good hold on a rock and then find a firm toehold before pulling myself up. The rock feels hot and solid in my hands. Unlike hiking, I now engage all my muscles to move up the mountain. It's a true workout: *I love workouts!* My heart pounds in my ears, from the exertion and the excitement. There's nothing boring about this ascent.

On this steeper slope, we gain elevation with great speed. Through the summer, I've learned to love the calm of hiking, the uneventful hours blurring into each other, but I abandon that calmness easily, drawn to this turn toward excitement. *This is adventure! This is fun!* But my body tells me something else too — something that has nothing to do with adventure or fun.

Jowita's edgy big city energy fuels her climb. With her long lean body, she scrambles up this nearly vertical slope like an eight-legged bug.

"Jowita," I yell straight above me, where she stretches her long body to its full reach, pulling herself up to the next level of rock. "Be careful! Falling is not an option here, hey?"

I think I hear an affirmative response, but she does not pause in her race upward.

"It's like addiction," I yell. "Like drinking. *Falling is not an option.*"

"I was thinking the same thing," she grunts as she drags herself over a rough slab.

I don't know about this idea. That's what the doubtful rumble in my gut tells me. I crank my neck, looking straight to the sky where I can catch a glimpse of the top of the mountain, a long rocky ridge against August's brightest blue. I know from our family hike earlier this summer that an easy, safe trail runs along that ridge. We can't be far. If we can just get up there, I tell myself, we should be able to — no, we *will* be able to — get back on the trail.

"See that ridge there? Above the treeline?" Jowita does not stop to look, but I keep yelling at her ascending back as I stretch for another rock hold. "We just gotta get there. We keep climbing. We'll pop out on top, get on the trail, and then we'll be fine." I hear my own confidence and ignore the inner voice, the one that says, *Right, Angie, because that is how mountains work — you just head in the "up direction" and then you "pop out" on top.*

Marty has told me the four stages of mountain adventure: cautious, confident, cocky, crash. I would add "comfortable" to bridge the big gap between "cautious" and "confident." I took years to get from cautious to comfortable and then another solid summer of hiking to get from comfortable to confident. I briefly wonder if I am suddenly progressing through the latter two stages at a much faster pace.

I stretch my hand as high as I can, until my toes barely touch the rock below me. Feeling the reach pull my torso and legs tight, I yank myself up, knowing I cannot fall. My body hates me for being here. I recognize the feeling. I am a kid on the highest diving tower at the local pool, and I do not want to jump. My body refuses to leap, but I am too afraid to walk back down the ladder. *Get me out of here.* That's what my body has to say about this adventure.

Jowita doesn't seem to share my hesitation. She's a spider scurrying up the rock face. "Hey, Jowita," I yell up the mountain. "Just so you know — the first aid kit is in my backpack. If you need it."

"Okay," Jowita answers in monosyllables, her voice hollow. Oh-kay. We're not joyful and laughing now. Jowita doesn't slow at all, and I'm having trouble keeping up. *What's the race?* We haven't rested since the younger women passed us. We haven't paused even a moment to think. Originally, we might have hoped to catch those two, but I've let go of that expectation. They're not here. Nobody would be here. Except us.

I'm sweating hard now, the itch of warm liquid nagging at my hairline. I tug my shirt away from my skin and let the breeze cool me. The sun burns the back of my shoulders. I'm not in a good spot to rest and have a drink; instead, I do what we've been doing for over an hour: I keep going.

I can barely reach the next handhold, but I grunt through the ascent, scratching an elbow as I drag myself up the rough rock. Blood runs down my arm. "Jowita, slow down for a second," I yell. "Let me get a look." She does stop for a brief time, but before I gain much distance on her, she's scurrying up the slope again. I keep yelling. She keeps scurrying.

Each reach and pull up the mountainside gets more treacherous, risky, and frightening. I jam my knee into an abrasive stone to pull myself safely over a tricky part, and blood trickles down my shin. I watch the bright red run a path through thick black dirt and down my lower leg. I repeat my new mantra: *falling is not an option*.

Bleeding we can survive. Falling we might not. Jowita and I are both good at not drinking. We decide not to drink, and we don't drink, most of the time. Now, we will decide not to fall, and we will not fall.

I say all these reassuring words to myself, repeatedly, but my body has begun to shake. It's not a shiver, because I'm not cold, but a persistent low-grade quake in my arms and my legs. A vibration in my chest and in my brain. While my mind says *falling is not an option, do not fall,* my body sends a different message. My body says: *lady, you are fucked; you need to get out of here!*

"Jowita." I say her name with urgency, trying to communicate that our adventure has taken a serious turn. "Stop for a minute. Let me get my bearings." I just need one minute to think, but our friendship is too new. We're being overly polite with each other. If I were with Marty, I'd yell: *Fuck, Marty! Stop right now! I'm not moving.*

But Jowita keeps moving, and I keep following. Between stretching myself thin, belly pressed against rock, I take brief moments to scan the area for other options. The farther we go, the more our options narrow. We can't go back down the way we've come up. It's been hard enough ascending. Neither of us has the climbing skills to descend. We'd have to go down backward, like climbing down a ladder. I do not have the nerve. We would end up trying to crabwalk our way down. Potentially fatal. If we could climb out of this groove in the rock, we might be able to get onto the land to our left. We're above the treeline now, but the ground on that left side is still green. We might be able to switchback our way through the foliage to the top, where I imagine the trail to be.

It'll be okay. We'll pop out on top. We'll be okay.

This faux confidence does not trick me. A mountain is not a controlled environment. Jowita and I are not at a theme park. We've been issued no safety guarantees. If we get hurt, there's nobody to sue. Pictures of my accomplished mountaineering friends pop into my mind, each of them announcing, *It's not Disneyland, Angie.*

"Jowita! What about if we climb out of this —" this crevice or drainage or I don't even know what to call this feature we're in. I am no mountain expert. "— this . . ." This fucking hole is what I want to say. "— we climb out of this *fissure*, and we get onto that . . . *green part*. The green looks less steep. We could make our way up there."

My self-confidence has been misplaced, I see it so clearly now, and I have dragged my city friend into the resulting crash. Cautious, comfortable, confident, cocky, crash.

Is this the "confidence" I've been working so hard to push Katie toward, only one easy misstep from its dangerous "cocky" cousin? And what if I had brought Katie with us today? If she had wanted to come, I *would* have brought her.

"You want to go over there?" Jowita shoots me an incredulous glance. She doesn't loosen either hand from the rocks above her, but she points her chin at the greenery. "There? No. I'm not."

"No. Yes. Jowita. I really think we need to. That's what we have to do — get to the green part." Despite my calm tone, I know my repetition betrays me. I have pinned all my hopes on getting to the green part. "Then we can make our own switchbacks. We can ease our way up there through a less steep route, and we can get up to that ridge. The trail *must* be along that ridge. I've done this mountain before. I know exactly where we are."

Again, Jowita looks over her shoulder, down the steep angle to me, her body as tense as an athlete in the starting blocks. I know by now she won't stop her upward movement for long, not long enough for me to catch her. "I am *not* going out there." She says the words slowly, her face rigid. She means it: she will not go out there. I picture the Jowita of only a few days ago, flexing, her smile popping with her bicep, her story about making her own bed in the woods: this is not the same Jowita.

"You're scared?" I ask gently. Everything has been moving too fast. *We* have been moving too fast. Explorer Jon Turk has told me that most tragedies in the wild are social, dependent upon a combination of personalities that lead to poor decisions. I need to stop and assess our situation: where are we, how are we, what should we do.

Jowita does not answer my question. She does not tell me whether she feels scared. She whips her face back around to the rock and sets her limbs in motion. I cannot catch her.

I see now that her speed grows out of her fear. She thinks if she can simply keep going fast enough, she will get out of this mess. She will emerge somewhere safe where she does not need to be afraid.

When I finally catch Jowita, she has come to a stop only because she has reached a towering wall. She sits with her back pushed into the stone, her knees pulled into her chest. We are very high. She looks terrified. I force an artificial calm. "It's beautiful," I say. "Look." Rocky ridges, sharp peaks, and thick forest surround us in every direction, all through a brilliant filter of perfect midday sunshine, the silence absolute. Jowita does not look. Jowita does not seem the least bit interested in beauty. She stares at her running shoes.

"You stay here," I tell her, as if she might move, as if she hasn't already petrified into the rock face behind her. "I'm going to look around, see if I can spot the trail."

"Angie." Her voice roots me to the spot. I've never heard her so serious. "I'm scared. We need to call for help. I don't think you should move anywhere. It's not safe."

"It's fine. I think we're okay. Let me have a look." I pause. "It'd be so embarrassing, Jowita, to call for help and find out we're only twenty meters from the trail. Let me just look."

I can only move a few meters in either direction from where Jowita crouches at the rock wall. I step gingerly on the steep, loose scree. My body won't let me stand upright, so I walk in an awkward crouch, placing each foot carefully across the slope before taking the next step, my arms stiff out at my sides as if I'm walking a balance beam. I resist the wobble in my ankles, my knees, my hips.

"Angie! Be careful!" Jowita's voice is high with concern. "Please!"

I regulate my own voice before answering. "It's fine. I know exactly where we are. I just need to see the trail." I angle my feet across the scree, not letting them point down at the forest, miles below us. If I think about slipping here, I will faint or puke or both.

I should not be standing upright here.

I should not climb above Jowita.

But that's what happens, I climb above her and move slowly from one side to the other, covering the terrain available to me, willing a trail to appear. Seeing nothing, no way out, I inch my way back toward Jowita and sit down in the scree a meter above her. I dial Marty's work number, planning to keep my voice low enough that Jowita won't hear my concern. The call goes straight to his voicemail.

"Sorry, I'm not at my desk right now, but if you leave a message . . ."

As soon as I start talking to this machine, the bravado I have been maintaining for Jowita dissolves. My voice has a childish tremor. I could cry, but won't let myself. "Hi, Marty. It's Angie." I stop. What do I even say? "Jowita and I are hiking. You know that.

Well, we lost the trail. I don't know how. It kind of . . . ended. Then there was this other thing. Not a trail but like a trail. We followed that. We shouldn't have. We should have turned back, but we kept going . . . for far too long. Now we're way up high. Jowita is scared. We have cell service. I mean obviously, because you can hear me. Jowita wants to call 911 for help. But I'm not sure. We might be right by the trail. What if help comes and . . . ? I mean, god, that would be so embarrassing. But . . . I can't see any trail and . . . well, it's steep. Really steep. Jowita has good reason to be scared." I do not say that I am scared too. "I don't know what to do, Marty." I pause and take a deep shaky breath. "You can't help from there, I know. But . . . I don't know what to do. Sorry. I already said that. Call me." I listen to the dead air until I realize I have nothing else to say, and then I hang up.

"Give me a minute to think," I say for the third time. "Not moving, not talking, only thinking. I need some space to figure this out." Jowita and I sit side by side with sharp scree scraping the back of our legs. We lean back into the vertical rock face, our feet braced against the steep slope. We are very small, two tiny flecks on the side of a massive mountain, nothing but trees and rocks and sky whichever way we look. Jowita says nothing. I feel the sunburn rising on my chest and nose. We still have water. "Make sure you're drinking," I say. "I have lots of water if you run out." I scan the miles and miles of forest, hoping this time I will catch a glimpse of a trail and a safe route to it. Jowita does not reply but pulls out her water bottle and takes a long drink. She gives me time to think, as I requested.

My thinking does nothing to improve our situation.

"Angie, we really need to call for help. This isn't good."

"I called Marty."

"Marty?" I hear the absurdity as soon as she says his name. "What's Marty going to do?"

It's a fair question, with no hint of malice. *What is Marty going to do?*

"Okay. I think if we can get over onto the green part, off this rock, we can ease our way up in switchbacks, get to the ridge, find the trail." I'm stuck on this plan, and she's stuck in her one response to it.

"I don't think so," she says quietly. "With the shrubs . . . we can't even see the ground . . . there could be holes . . . if we fall here . . . not a good idea."

"It's not as steep as it looks. I promise. Watch me, and you'll see. Watch how I do it. Then copy me."

I ease my way out of the rocky crack onto the green side of the mountain. As soon as I'm out there, I realize it's steeper than it looks. I can't stand. I'm down on the ground, gripping the green and brown roots so tight they cut into my hands. My feet dangle below me with no hold. I'm belly to the mountain. If the roots let loose from their rocky soil, I will slide to my death, leaving Jowita alone with no idea how to tell anyone where to find her.

"Fuck," I say calmly. "Okay now I *am* scared." It feels good to say it aloud. I hold onto the foliage as tight as I can, checking that I have a handful of different root systems so if one gives, I've still got the other. The only direction I can possibly move is down. Using only my arms, moving from clutched root to clutched root, I aim to lower myself to a small flat spot twelve feet below. My triceps and biceps ache. The free fall beneath my feet makes me want to rest my cheek in the dirt and sob. "Okay . . . okay . . . okay . . .

okay," I whisper to myself with each inch of descent. "Okay . . . okay . . . okay . . . okay."

I am vaguely aware of Jowita on the phone above me, calling for help. "My address? *My* address is in Toronto. I don't see how that — yes — no, I heard you — we are *on a mountain* — no, I don't know — My address? In Toronto? You want my address in Toronto? — Okay. My address in Toronto is —"

"Yes, call for help," I think. "Please call for help." I am no longer worried about being embarrassed.

When I get to safe ground, Jowita lets me rest for a few moments before yelling down the mountain, "What did Marty say? When you called him?"

"I got his answering machine." I bite my lip against inappropriate laughter. Hilarity boils in my gut. I cannot let myself laugh, or cry. If I start, I won't stop.

"His answering machine," Jowita echoes. Despite her evident fear, she's close to laughter too.

I am comfortable on my natural grassy bench cut into the mountainside. The flat spot gets me out of immediate danger, but as I assess, I realize I have nowhere from here to go. The rocks slope at a deadly angle in every direction.

I let the situation sink in: my friend and I are in a terrible, rotten mess. This mess is my fault. "Hey, Jowita," I yell without turning to look up at her. "You were right. The green part is not less steep than it looks."

I take a video of the view to calm myself. There is no better scene on Earth. I post the video to Facebook with the comment: *Fuck. Help.* I click off Facebook and into my texting app and write Marty:

Don't worry. Everything is fine. Jowita called 911. Search and Rescue is on its way. I go back to Facebook and delete my post. I stare at the trees, reminding myself of their beauty, of how few people have seen them from here. Now would be a good time to unself.

"Jowita?"

"Yeah?"

"Do you think you could make it to where I am? It's a perfect bench. Enough room for both of us. Exactly two-bums wide. More comfortable and less exposed than where you are. Safe, once you get to it. It's so beautiful here. You have to use your arms, hold tight to the roots, lower yourself slowly. It's not that far. Then we can sit comfortably, together, and we can figure out what to do."

"I'll try."

I twist around and watch as she ties her green Adidas jacket around her waist with a double knot, shortens the straps on her little backpack and then, in a crabwalk, inches her way onto the green ground. She grips the roots, her face tight with fear. The tendons in her neck pop. I understand. Her instinct about my plan was correct in the first place. Why would she change her mind after she saw what happened to me? She barely makes it out of the crevice into the green. "No no no," she's saying. "No no." Then she's back into the rock funnel, getting sucked below me, and then out of my sight.

"Jowita!"

She's disappearing, and my phone is ringing. I answer. "Marty. Hold on. Jowita tried to get to me but she couldn't. Now she's down the mountain. In this . . . I don't know, rock thing. I can't see her. Hold on." I leave him listening as Jowita and I grow farther apart yelling back and forth to each other. When she assures me she's at a safe resting spot, I put my ear back to the phone.

"Hi," I say.

It's unbelievable that he's here, his voice so clear.

"Ang, what on Earth? I saw you'd called, but I was busy with meetings and didn't listen to your voice message. Then I got your text: *don't worry, search and rescue is on its way?* Okay — so that actually *does* worry me. What's going on?"

I catch him up. I've exhausted my everything-is-fine act on Jowita. I hear the way I talk to Marty, and I hate it. I sound weak. Later, when he tells the story, he will describe this phone call as the first time in our twenty-year relationship that he's ever heard me scared.

"Stay where you are," he tells me. "Do not move. Understand? Absolutely do not move. Wait for help."

If I stretch and lean to the far left, I can grab a glimpse of Jowita wedged between two rocks. *Hey, Jowita, you're between a rock and a hard place!*

She swipes her finger across her phone, top to bottom. Swipe, click. Swipe, click. The powerful sun reflects off its surface so the device shines from her palm. I yell down: "Purging your history?" At my house, we go to bed early, and I know Jowita has been entertaining herself on her phone long after we're all asleep. "A few pics to delete?"

"I do not want to be caught dead with this shit on my phone."

We laugh, but not easy and long like before. This time our laughter vibrates with nervous energy. It's a we-are-fucked laugh. A what-else-are-you-going-to-do-but-laugh laugh.

"Are you hot?" I ask because I am sweltering. *I'm dying of heat*, I might say in different circumstances.

"Yeah. There's no shade. I'm frying on this rock."

"Are you sitting somewhere comfortable, though?"

"No."

"Do you feel safe where you are?"

"Mmm. Maybe?"

"Should I try to come over there? So we can sit together?"

"No! Angie, don't, really. I'm on this root and then there's . . . well . . . it's . . . I don't . . . There's not room over here for both of us. I think it's . . . dangerous."

"Oh god," I say into my hands. I bite my finger to stop myself from laughing, aware that hysteria is lurking. "I'm so sorry."

"Is this where we call our kids and tell them we love them?"

"No. Jowita. We're going to be okay. Drink your water."

What's going on? The message pops up on my Facebook app. It's from Jowita's ex, her only child's father, a big city literary star who writes perfect, tight short stories. I have never met him.

Yet here he is: *What's going on?*

Oh, you know, not much. Just hanging. What's going on with you?

That's what I want to type. Instead, I write one word: *Sorry.* I pause, and then press send. I assume Jowita has given him the details. He has no other reason to write me. I wait for a while, knowing I need to tell him more. But what?

Finally, I type: *I think help is on its way. We'll be okay, I promise.*

"Jowita," I yell down the hill. "I got a note from your ex. Just to be clear on your whole arrangement: if I put him in *my* hiking memoir, do *I* have to give him a giant penis?"

I am so relieved to hear her laugh, full and true.

"Wait. He's back. He says *get J to read you my jokes.*"

"Oh they're so bad, Angie."

"Tell me anyway." She does and we laugh more than the jokes warrant. "We're going to be okay," I say again. "Are you scared?"

Jowita answers without hesitation: "I don't want to talk about that."

My phone rings. "Hello," I say, "Angie speaking." Casual and normal, as if I'm not roasting clutched to a mountain, nothing but one square meter of flat earth separating me from doom.

"Angie. Hello. I'm with Fernie Search and Rescue. Your friend phoned 911. That call for help has gone through all the appropriate channels and paperwork. It takes a while, but now I am here, ready to help. Tell me where you're at."

"I know exactly where we are." That's the first thing I say to him. I explain to him that though we're definitely stuck in some tricky terrain, I do know the way back down — we could descend exactly where we came up. "Should we do that?" I ask him. "Should we go back down the funnel we climbed up?"

"I'm not going to tell you to do that," he says, kindly. "I can't see the terrain. I don't want to say 'yes, climb down' and then have you hurt yourselves."

"That's how I feel. I could decide to climb down and then maybe we end up loosening rocks into each other's heads, because we can only go single file, it's narrow, or maybe my friend falls and breaks her leg, or worse."

We chat for maybe five minutes. Our conversation feels comfortable and relaxed. I could keep talking to him all day, so relieved am I to hand over responsibility. I don't know what about my turn of phrase or my tone alerts him, but suddenly he says "Do not move. We're coming to get you with a longline. A helicopter will fly by once to assess. Then it will land, and our guys will make a plan before coming back to retrieve you. Do not move." My line goes dead.

"Hi, Mom? It's Angie. Is Dad there? Okay, don't say anything aloud that he can hear. I don't want him to know what's going on. I'm not in the mood to hear his take on how stupid I've been. Just say yep, yep, yep. Jowita and I got ourselves in trouble. We're stuck on the mountain. I put a note on social media and then took it off, but I wanted to get in touch in case you saw it. Don't freak out. Help is coming. It's bad, but we'll be okay. Word gets around in a small town: I thought you might worry. Don't. I am very glad you didn't come with us, though. Oh god, and Katie. Thank goodness. Yeah, I know — yes . . . yes . . . okay . . . Okay. Bye."

"How long do you think the helicopter will be?"

"Oh no, Jowita, you sound terrible. Are you okay? Want me to throw some water down?"

"No, I'm alright." Jowita does not sound alright.

"They said forty to ninety minutes."

"How long has it been?"

"Maybe an hour? Not long now." Rocks rattle above my head. One slowly rolls toward Jowita. She screams as it hits her on the way down.

"Just my arm," she yells up to me. "I'm okay." I don't like the way she sounds, and I assess the slope between us once again, wishing for a way to traverse it.

"Ay-oh! Ay-oh!" I yell.

"What?! Why are you doing that?!"

"Nothing. I thought maybe people might be above us, knocking rocks."

"People?" Jowita does not believe me.

"Or something." *Please let it be mountain goats.*

I shift, becoming more alert to the constraint of this square meter. I have been staring at the same trees and peaks, reminding myself of their beauty, for over an hour. It's not working. I cannot believe we're stuck on the side of a mountain in cougar territory waiting to be rescued by a helicopter. I try not to dwell on the knowledge that blood attracts mountain lions. Jowita has her period. Until she arrived, I hadn't menstruated in months, but my body, never one to miss a party, synched right in with hers. Now we're both stuck here, bleeding. *Here, kitty kitty kitty.* "Ay-oh! Ay-oh," I yell at the shifting rocks above me. "Ay-oh!"

"More somethings?"

"I talked to Marty again. He called his helicopter pilot friend, Dave. It turns out Dave's the one coming. There will be a rope hanging off the helicopter and then — I don't know. We get on that."

"We get on the rope? The rope that will be hanging off the helicopter?"

"They're experts. They'll take care of us." I am terrified of heights. I wonder if I can let them rescue Jowita with the longline and then try to walk back down myself. Fuck. *"Jowita,"* I scream, filling my words with all my frustration and helplessness, *"this is not boring!! You promised to be boring!!"*

When the helicopter arrives, it does not come to us. We hear it approach: *it's coming, it's coming, it's coming.* Relief floods me: let this be over. Then the helicopter veers the other direction, flying circles around a peak very far away from us. I don't understand.

"It's not coming," Jowita says. "Why isn't it coming?"

Forcibly ignoring my vertigo, I stand up. As soon as I do, I understand. I have told them the wrong spot. *I know exactly where we are.* How many times have I said it?

Well. I have no idea where we are. I gently turn around to face the mountain and take a cautious half step back from the steep slope we've been attempting to climb. As easy as that one half step, our setting comes into perfect, clear focus. All along, I've been trying to get closer to get a good look, and all along I need to get farther away. With the new perspective, I see. The helicopter, a tiny housefly in the distance, is exactly where I *thought* we were. All the distinguishing features of the mountain we meant to climb are painfully clear, way over there, where I told them they'd find us. *That* is the ridge where I hoped we'd "pop out."

My phone rings. "I'm sorry —" I start talking before my SAR contact has any time to tell me that his guys can't find us. "We're not where I said I was. I don't understand. Maybe we're on . . ." Panic disorients me, and I start naming off mountains in the area, names that don't even make sense. I do know where we started the hike. That starting point limits the options of where we could've ended up in the space of a day. I should stop talking. Instead, I name every mountain I know.

"Listen, Angie" — he interrupts me in the kind of calming voice I learned to use back in my lifeguard days — "it's okay. You can see the helicopter. Tell me when it gets closer to you and when it gets farther away."

He guides me through the process of directing the helicopter to us. Even when it gets so close that its noise overpowers my voice, the pilot and the rescue personnel cannot spot us. "Everything is going to be alright," the man on the other end of my phone assures me. "Wave something bright. They will keep flying back around until they see you. You're small on a big mountain."

Jowita waves her green Adidas jacket. I wave my red long-sleeve polypro. We wave and wave and wave. It seems we could throw a rock and hit the damn helicopter, it's that close.

Finally, they see us.

Blue ropes dangle long below the helicopter. Two men hang in harnesses at the end of the ropes. Between them swings a third rope and an unfilled harness. *There's no fucking way I'm getting on that thing.*

I feel tremendous relief when the helicopter doesn't come for me. It hovers steady above Jowita, lowering slowly until the two men touch ground. I imagine they're attaching Jowita to the third harness, a giant diaper made of straps and wires, and double-checking buckles as they reassure her, but I can't see or hear any of it. I hear only the spinning rotor, and I cover my ears to its noise. With my hands occupied, my hair blows wild in the breeze of the rotors. I close my eyes against the sting of my own hair whipping me in the face. In less than five minutes, the helicopter lifts again, the noise gets farther and farther away. The air grows still. I watch Jowita's bare swinging legs get smaller and smaller until they're gone.

She forgot her sweatshirt. That's the main thing I notice. Her favorite green Adidas jacket. She untied it from her waist to wave the blast of color, to catch the pilot's attention. She must have left it on the rocks. I am not going to get it.

I send a Facebook message to Jowita's ex: *They just flew Jowita off the mountain in a harness, between two Search and Rescue guys, dangling from the bottom of a helicopter. I assume they're coming back for me. She's all good. I should've taken a video. I would've if I didn't feel so hysterical.*

He writes back: *Jesus good luck!*

As terrified as I am of heights, I feel nothing but relief when that longline lifts me off the mountain. The two rescue guys ask if I'm scared. They're maybe in their thirties — one with short blond hair and a full arm of tattoos, the other with moppy hair and a scruffy mountain-man beard. I wonder how much time has to pass before I can joke with Jowita about my exemplary hosting efforts, going the extra mile to arrange her an airlift with a couple of hot men. I'm strapped into a secure harness, and the two rescuers hang on either side of me. I feel surprisingly safe. "No. I'm fine actually. It's pretty."

"Good. We have hoods we put over people's faces when they're real scared. Screamer bags."

"I don't need a screamer bag." I smile. "This is beautiful."

They point to their ears and wave me to stop talking. The pilot slowly flies us off the mountain and over the forest and way down to a little lake in the far distance. It's a long ride.

As we approach the lake, the guy with the beard yells, "We're going to drop you near the edge of the water. Once we undo your harness, run to the picnic table where your friend is sitting and then Dave will land the helicopter. You can get in, and he'll fly you both back to town."

Our ordeal has not detracted from Jowita's glamor. She's stunning there in the wilderness, cross-legged in her denim cut-offs and dirty white tank top, her hand lifted to her mouth.

"Are you smoking a cigarette?" I ask as she jumps off the table and runs to greet me with a forceful hug.

"No!" She holds her hand out to show me a half-eaten juicy peach.

"In the book, it's going to be a cigarette." Our laughter is giddy and high. We're not okay.

"Look at you!" I point at Jowita's bloody knees, her dirty face and elbows. Turning around, I tuck up the back of my shorts to show her my legs and ass, rubbed raw, my skin still clinging to the mountain.

"Don't even." She shifts her leg to show me her backside, red and bleeding like mine. In Lori Lansens's *The Mountain Story*, a character misses the last tram of the day and, miscalculating the steepness of the mountain, decides he can walk down. He ends up inching his way down the slope on his rear end. The friction of the slide burns his pants and underwear right off his body. The soles of his boots disappear, and he nearly scrapes off his whole ass. He undergoes years of skin grafts and still can never again put any weight on his left butt cheek. That would have been us, if Jowita hadn't called for help. If we got lucky.

"Thanks," Jowita says to the rescue guy closest to us, the blond with the full sleeve tattoo.

"Oh." He shrugs, one side of his mouth curling up in a smirk. "It was no problem."

"Really? It *seemed*," Jowita laughs, "like a problem."

By the time we get home, a press release has already appeared online. I think I might barf when I see the little red circles that mark Jowita and me, up high on the mountain, together but apart. I look where I walked up above the circles, trying to spot the trail, and I think I might faint. I force a lightness I don't feel, just as I did on the mountain. People come and go from our house all evening, writer friends wanting to say goodbye to Jowita before her early morning departure for Ontario. They knew our day's plans, and they saw the incident report on the Search and Rescue Facebook page. They've made the connection; everyone wants to hear the story. Jowita and I tell it over and over again, making it a little funnier each time.

"Hey, Ollie, remember when you told me about the grade six trust walk at your school? You said, 'Who would let twelve-year-old boys take each other on a trust walk?' You walked Jesse right into the lake! Well, today I took Jowita on a trust walk." With laughter, we sidestep the true precariousness of our situation. We cannot yet face it head-on.

"You should start your own guiding company, Ang." Marty plays to the audience. "Every hike ends in a helicopter ride!"

"Anybody can offer helicopter rides," I counter. "I offer *longline* rides."

"A helicopter . . ." Katie pouts. "I wish I would've come."

"Oh. Katie. God. No."

After the guests go home and Marty and I retreat to our bedroom, my phone dings with a text from Jowita: *That was the best day of my life. I'm not even joking. I can't explain why yet. Thank you.*

I lift the screen toward Marty. "I'm so relieved she doesn't hate me."

That night, I wake in terror. There in the dark, with nobody laughing, my body acknowledges how badly the day could have gone. I'm gripping roots on the mountainside, face to the dirt, no safety net between me and death. Buzzing and alert, I feel the panic of my feet hanging in nothing but air. I see my friend — dirty and bruised and cut, clinging to a mountain that she would not even be able to find on a map, depending entirely on me. Panic sears right through my bones. I roll into Marty's warm, sleeping body. "I'm scared," I say into the space between his neck and shoulder, "so very scared."

By the next morning, people online are busy making fun of Jowita and me. The SAR Facebook page describes the rescue, saying "the couple" did the right thing when they called for help. *The right thing would've been to not be out there in the first place*, one guy writes. Elsewhere somebody heckles: *I hope those two imbeciles are paying for that little helicopter ride.* Anxiety rises in my chest. More of the same wherever I look.

"I can't believe my response," I tell Jowita, shoving my phone in my pocket. "So intensely physical. As if I'm more afraid of strangers being mean to me online than I was of falling off that fucking mountain."

But I don't engage.

I put my phone down and walk away from it. This is what I have learned. Maybe I do need to have an online presence. Maybe I do need to be on social media. When I first started Twitter, my profile read: *making up for a real absence with a virtual presence.* I rely on that presence, professionally. I live 2,756 kilometers from Toronto, the publishing center of Canada. I can't afford to let people there forget I exist. I need to maintain connections with those colleagues and friends. I want to. Even Cal Newport, the author of *Deep Work* and advocate for staying off social media, has modified his stance. Initially, he argued we don't need these e-worlds. Truly important work and original thinking come from sustained focus, he said, and social media platforms only distract us from that necessary immersion. He sang the praises of working when we work and, when we don't have to work, staying offline. (Read a newspaper! Watch a baseball game!) Now he argues, instead, to make that social media difficult to access. Put social media accounts on a different computer, an old one that doesn't work that well, one with hard-to-remember passwords. Put that computer on a hard-to-reach shelf in an out-of-the-way closet. Don't make it easy to slip onto social media in every lull. Then when we really need to get on it, we can — but we don't do so out of boredom or procrastination or habit.

I'm not where Cal Newport is, obviously, but I'm moving in that direction. If Marty and I go on a date night, he takes his phone so I can leave mine at home. If I know the kids can reach us through him, I don't need my phone. Same if we go hiking together — he takes his phone for emergencies. I leave mine in the glove compartment. When I do scroll through my social media accounts or engage with online comments, I listen to my body. As soon as those hyperactive butterflies start to stir in my gut, I put my phone facedown in a dark corner, and I walk away from it. This is what I have learned. This is what I can teach my kids. An e-device is a tool. Use it when it serves you. Know when to put it away. Stay vigilant. Listen to your body. Don't let yourself be drawn to the e-world's promise of constant stimulation.

The week after Jowita goes home to Toronto, my iPhone rings. I forget these things work as plain old telephones. I hesitate, but I answer. The man on the other end of the line identifies himself as a member of Fernie Search and Rescue. "I heard people have been harassing you online. The good old internet. I wanted to tell you not to worry about it. You did the right thing. You gave us an easy rescue. Too often people wait too long, and we have to execute a rescue in the dusk, or — even less ideal — people have to spend the night outside, waiting for a morning rescue. Often, people wait until they're hurt, out of water, or disoriented. That complicates the situation too. You made the rescue smooth for us by calling when you did. There are so many ways the day could have gone much worse. Your friend was hanging onto a root just above a pebbly slide to a fatal fall. You needed help. That's the point of Search and Rescue. Nobody makes fun of someone calling the Fire Department because their house is on fire or the Police Station because they've been robbed. That kind of online harassment is dangerous if it stops people from calling SAR when they need us."

After my last two years of judgment and criticism, his kindness moves me to tears. That someone would take time out of his day to tell me that I didn't do anything wrong feels impossibly generous. Warmth fills me, a sensation I recognize as gratitude. "Thank you," I say. "Really — thank you."

A good hike is a boring hike. In retrospect, my summer outdoors has been delightfully boring, all except the one day that Jowita and I decided to "do something big." I save Jowita's text and read it daily over the next few weeks: *That was the best day of my life. I'm not even joking. I can't explain why yet. Thank you.*

Gradually, I can explain the euphoria, the thrill of coming close to dying and therefore feeling, vividly, the immense gift of life. We grew more alive because of our brush with death.

Jowita tells me that back in Toronto, her heart speeds up every time she sees a helicopter. "They make me so happy, helicopters," she says. "I love them."

I have a similar feeling each time I see Dave, the helicopter pilot. When he walks into a room, I feel flooded with relief, starting in my heart and spreading through my limbs. *Oh good, Dave is here. Everything will be okay.*

I will never forget our day on that mountain. People ask me, "Does Jowita still talk to you?" I assure them the mistakes of that day — its terror — did not drive us apart. Rather we bonded over our shared experience, friends forever.

Ultimately, though, I decide I do not feel the same as Jowita does. I will carry this experience with me always, but our helicopter rescue does not make the long list of my life's best days. I would rather pick our day taking the safe route, away from the moose, or our day walking around a spring-fed lake.

I understand being jacked up on the drama of the rescue, but I do not need that excitement anymore. I don't even want it. At fifty, I will, every single time, choose a long, boring walk over sexy rescue guys and a longline helicopter ride.

Give me the trees, the silence, the sore feet, the long hours. Give me serenity.

Give me boredom.

Ten

Like a Girl to Water

"**K**atie. Stop." Ollie pronounces each word with force, his voice stern. I would say the same — *Katie! Stop!* — but instead I direct all my energy to paddling. "This is *not* fun," he scolds. "This is *serious*."

Katie, of course, disagrees with her brother. She laughs, delighted, while our red canoe rides high on the swell of another white-capped wave. I wipe my inner elbow across my eyes as the canoe's belly slaps down in the wave's trough, splashing more water in my face.

"This is so stupid. We're all going to die. The shore isn't getting any closer."

I want to glance behind me, where Ollie frets, to make sure he's not gripping the boat's gunwales, ensuring we'll capsize. I don't dare turn; I only paddle. I have to trust that Marty — from where he steers in the stern — will be the one to notice and react if the kids make any moves to put us in greater danger. I focus on stabbing the dragon, forcing my paddle into the dark heart of each wave.

The water is black and cold, glacier fed, and there is an awful lot of it. We're on one of the biggest, deepest lakes in British Columbia, 104 kilometers in length, up to 152 meters deep, and three to five kilometers wide. We've picked a narrow section to cross, but still we can barely see the other side.

"It's not stupid!" Katie shouts loud above the wind and the crashing water. "It's *awesome*! I love it! Wheeeee!" My girl is high on adrenaline, the only one of us completely oblivious to the risk.

"Katie. I am serious. Stop. The shoreline isn't any closer. Mom, why isn't the shoreline getting any closer?"

"Okay," I intervene, without letting up on my paddle stroke, without turning even slightly in their direction. "Both of you, stop. This is not the time for second-guessing. No negative thoughts. Let's focus on moving forward. The shore *is* getting closer." I think. I mean, it *must* be.

A good time for second-guessing would have been an hour ago, before we set out.

"Let's do it. It's not as bad as it looks," Marty had assured me.

I laughed. "Oh no no. I have fallen for that trick of nature already this summer. I bet it actually is precisely as bad as it looks. If not worse."

"We can just try."

So, with our canoe too full, loaded with enough gear, gadgets, beer, and books to ensure a long weekend of luxury camping, we tried. As soon as we steered into the open water, the boat lurched and swayed, more in the weather's control than ours. Marty, for once, agreed with me, and we steered back to shore, to wait out the wind.

After forty minutes of pacing the rocky beach, Marty announced that the water had calmed enough to give the crossing a second go. I squinted out to the middle of the giant lake. "There are still white-caps out there."

"Nah, it's an optical illusion, just the setting sun glinting off the top of the waves."

Is this an optical illusion? That's what I want to ask Marty now, our overloaded canoe bouncing around in these terrifying waves, Katie squealing like she's at Disneyland while Ollie forecasts the end of our time on planet Earth. *Is this "the sun glinting off the waves," Marty?*

I zip my mouth and paddle hard. The more intensely I work, the faster I will get us out of this deathtrap. Marty does a good job of steering, making sure the waves don't broadside us, and I do a good job of sprinting. We find a rhythm: paddle, paddle, upswing, coast, slap, splash; paddle, paddle, upswing, coast, slap, splash. Ollie and Katie turn their attention to bickering about whether the shoreline seems to be getting closer or farther away. I try to ignore them as I continually map out our shortest emergency route to land, in case we need to swim. I paddle as if my children's lives depend on my effort.

By the time we pull into the campsite, the sun has set, and the wind begins to weaken. The spot where we plan to pitch our tent sits empty, but a lone shadow of a man stands on the beach, securing his sailboat from the windstorm. A sliver of smoke from his campfire rises over the trees on the backside of this little bay.

He shakes his head. "A canoe," he says. "I've been watching you. I told my girlfriend, 'I think it's a canoe.' But she said, 'No, no way.' A canoe," he says again. "You guys are fucking crazy."

Friends with a little motorboat and a child a few years younger than ours always celebrate Labour Day weekend at this quiet campsite with its white-sand beach and cold, clear water. We don't do motorsports, but, on a last-minute whim, we decided to make the ambitious paddle over to join them for these last days of summer. They're less concerned about a late-night crossing in their sturdier vessel and come motoring into shore once we already have our tent up and our fire roaring.

Even in a motorboat, they pull up to the beach pumped full of adrenaline. "That's a sporty one tonight! We had a few close calls. Can't believe you guys did that in a canoe."

"Maybe a bit more planning for the return trip," Marty concedes. "Our best bet will probably be early in the morning. This lake can be calm as glass. I've seen it."

"Enough with the risks," I agree. "That's my second narrow escape in a week."

Over the weekend, I run into the couple camping around the bend a few times, either collecting water at the stream or coming and going from the sole outhouse. Eventually the man quits shaking his head at me ("a *canoe*?!") and tells me his stories about outings gone wrong on this dangerous, unpredictable waterbody. My heart pounds in my ears as I listen to his account of a man and woman capsizing last summer.

"This section of lake isn't covered under the jurisdiction of any emergency response teams or Search and Rescue," he tells me. "Nobody could come get the couple. The two of them made it to the shore, wet and cold, and then retreated to the outhouse, wrapped themselves in toilet paper and hid in the shitter until the weather calmed and someone in a motorboat happened upon the site to help them. They spent *days* in that outhouse."

"Toilet paper," Ollie repeats, his eyes popping. "See?!"

But Katie is not there to see. She's already toddled off in search of more danger. She and her dad have found the perfect cliff-jumping spot.

"Katie. Cliff jumping? Marty? Really? With her broken arm?" Katie crashed in the bike park last weekend, chasing her cousin down a particularly steep run-in to a jump. Now she wears a neon pink cast, wrist to elbow.

"The doctor said I could." Katie cocks her hip to the side, hand on her waist. She wears a bright pink one-piece swimsuit, but she's mostly long white limbs. Her undercut has grown out over the summer, and a mass of tangled auburn curls hangs almost to her shoulders. She flicks her head to get the wet strands of hair out of her eyes. "The *doctor* specifically said the cast is *waterproof*."

"I think, Katie, sweetheart, the doctor said that to give you the okay for *showering*. Not for cliff jumping."

Marty, fully on Team Cliff Jump, wins this argument. He and Katie jog across the beach to climb the steep black rocks jutting out above deep, clear water. I lean against the canoe, its belly warm in the sun, dig my toes into the sand, and prepare to spend a long, hot day reading. "Just be careful," I yell at their backs. "Please."

Ollie pauses to look at me for a moment. "Really," he says. "You think this is a good idea? Really?" He shakes his head, his cheeks puffing out with the force of his sigh, and then he follows them.

I read Spinoza. A colleague has tipped me off to the work, particularly a book called *Ethics*, in which Spinoza argues that nature and God are synonyms. Spinoza says everything in the universe is part of nature or God, terms that are — to his mind — interchangeable.

All is nature; all is God. I wonder if my cottonwood and Aristotle's thaumazein and Murdoch's unselfing and Spinoza's theory of nature-as-God are all nibbling at the same idea — that sense of connection and wonder and meaning that we can find in nature when we allow ourselves full immersion. Echoing Spinoza, Iris Murdoch describes these divine sensations in nature as a relaxing of the spirit "into the shared pulse of existence." I *know* that shared pulse. I have felt it when gazing through my bedroom window at my friendly giant cottonwood. The pulse tapped at my neck as I watched Katie, spellbound on a mountaintop. I felt the pulse again while I trekked alone for eleven hours through cougar country. I even felt that shared pulse of existence as I dug my nails into the steep slope of a mountain, my cheek hard against the scree, while Jowita called 911.

Wanting some weekend reading a little lighter than Spinoza, I have also brought a novel about a young woman coming out to her family as a lesbian in 1980s' Calgary. I fall in love with this character, Nancy Jo Cullen's Frankie, mostly for the resoluteness with which Frankie knows herself. No matter how poorly her family and friends react, Frankie does not doubt who she is, does not waver, does not try to change, for anybody. She might feel disappointment in how others receive her, but she has a rock-solid core of Frankie-ness that remains untouched by this disappointment. Frankie is well suited to the 1980s, a time before social media. Cullen's Frankie would have no patience for the idiocy of Facebook, the way it pushes its users to seek praise, as if we engage in each experience not for pleasure or personal growth, but for the sake of external affirmation that we live worthwhile, enviable lives. We interrupt the experience of hiking, racing online to post pictures, abandoning the real world for the virtual one in a bid to win likes. Frankie doesn't need this kind of approval. As a literary creation, she seems fully alive and fully herself *because* of her lack of need. I vow to be more like Frankie. Lounged in my bed of sand, I revel in Cullen's clever, sharp writing. The short chapters give me plenty of opportunity to jump in the cold water to refresh. I race Katie freestyle across the bay, join her for a jump or two, and then lean back into the hot red of the canoe, and relax with my books.

I alternate between rooting for Frankie and decoding Spinoza, pleasurably dragging out the experience of each. I don't pick up my phone once all weekend, don't share the details of our days on social media. I decide, instead, to save the best of my family and my life for ourselves. I focus on living our lives rather than narrating them. I don't need any likes to know my good fortune.

Katie pops by in breaks from her adventures and engages me in conversation. She's full of life, happy to spend the weekend in her bathing suit, running around the beach, racing our friends' son into the water, swimming out to climb on a big rock twenty meters from shore, or leaping off the higher cliff with her dad.

"You've gotta take a break from the water and let your cast dry out," I nag her.

"The doctor said —"

"The doctor said your cast could be wet for *twenty minutes*. Remember? I was there."

"But I'm not staying in the lake for more than twenty minutes." Katie does this now — challenges me, sticks fast to her view of the world rather than being malleable to mine.

"Yes, Katie, but you're in and out of the water *all day*. You have to give the cast a chance to dry." I already know we'll be getting a new cast on Tuesday. I'll be paying too — both in cash and in a lecture from the physician tasked with removing this soggy mess. No parenting awards for me this weekend.

Katie looks so happy, though, so full and alive. I cannot bring myself to clip her wings.

"Oh, Katie," I sigh. "Just be careful. Be smart."

"Kat," she says, climbing on the canoe behind me, straddling it like a horse, her long white leg with its scabby knee, dangling at my ear.

"What?"

"Kat. I'm changing my name. I don't like 'Katie' anymore. Katie is a bit . . . too young for me. I'm going to be called Kat now."

I pause for a moment, startled by my youngest child's decisiveness. "Kat? Okay. I like it. It suits you." I tilt my head to get a good look at this new girl, this *Kat*. "Let's hope you have nine lives like a real cat. And that you always land on your fee—"

"Mom. Not that kind of cat. With a K."

I have given her three names (Katherine Elizabeth Jean), plus a nickname (Katie). Today, she sheds them all and chooses her own. I slide my back down the canoe and lie flat in the sand, enjoying the warm sun drying my skin. I loop a finger around my girl's toe as I smile and close my eyes. "Nice to meet you, Kat." I remember Ollie doing the same around the same age. At nine, he declared Ollie a "baby name" and switched to Oliver. He floated between the two for a while and then settled back into Ollie. I wonder if Kat will stick.

The silence hangs between my daughter and me for several minutes, and I assume Kat will race off to join our friends' son at water's edge, but she stays, banging her loose heel against the ribs of the canoe while letting me keep my hold on her other foot. "Mom," she finally says, "you know what I hate? I hate when teachers and other adults say that it's going to be up to me and my generation to fix all the mess of the world. Like, they know we're just kids, right? Not even teenagers yet. I mean, can't *you guys* fix it?"

Ooof.

She's copying Ollie. I know that. He said almost the same thing, word for word, at the end of school in June. Have these phrases been playing around in my daughter's head since then? All summer?

Can't you guys fix it?

My girl does this lately — the mimicking — as if she's trying on ideas to see whether or not they suit her. She's gradually creating her own Kat worldview. Twice this weekend, I've heard my words in her mouth, forcing me to realize how vigilant I need to be of the example I set.

I don't know what to say to this question about the world and its mess and who will fix it and how. "Climate change," I ask tentatively, "is that what you mean? The environmental mess?"

"Well, that, and . . . yeah —" She wrinkles her nose. "Mostly. Environment."

The summer has packed her face full of freckles. I wish I could make light of her question, suggest that instead of addressing such an adult topic, we try to count her freckles, like we used to do when she was little. One million and one, one million and two, one million and . . . "That can all get pretty depressing, Kati— I mean, Kat! If you think of it too much," I say slowly, knowing I furrow my brow as I try to find an answer for her. "But we also can't ignore it. We do *all* have to *try* to fix it. You know what I've been pondering lately . . ." I pause to see if she's still interested. She slides off the canoe and joins me in the sand, lying flat so that our shoulders touch. She waits. "My back is really bad, right? From my car accidents? My spine is all kind of cracked and deteriorating. I guess I sort of knew that already, but when I actually *saw* the damage on an X-ray, I got more worried, thinking about my future, wondering if soon I'll be in too much pain, the kind that's hard to tolerate, or if my injuries will stop me from participating in activities that I love or from having the kind of life I want." I lace my fingers through hers as I talk. Hers are still cool from the lake. She lets me hold them. "Do you see, though, that nothing has changed except my knowledge? My back was exactly the same before the X-rays as it is afterward. But I could easily let the knowledge make me less happy and make me enjoy my life less, worrying about my future. Does my being less happy do anything at all to help my damaged spine?"

I roll my ear toward the sand, watching her reaction.

She shakes her head, solemn.

"No. Not at all. So instead . . . I guess I just . . . I do what I can to keep my spine healthy — be active, stretch, do some strength training. Otherwise, I try not to dwell on knowledge that makes me too sad." I lift her fingers toward my face, kiss the back of her hand. "It's like that with the planet too. We can't always live in that scary knowledge of what might be coming, worst-case scenarios. We can do our best to take care of our natural world, not abuse it, make it healthier, and then we can — in a safe, smart way — enjoy what's good."

I realize as I hear my words pour out how much time I have devoted to thinking about this topic, how ready I am for one of my kids to ask. I know the pull to apathy and despair.

What difference can I possibly make as one person with one small life?

Or, worse: *It's too late. We're doomed.*

I do not want to model that apathy or despair for my children. In *Learning to Die: Wisdom in the Age of Climate Crisis*, Robert Bringhurst writes, "You, your species, your entire evolutionary family, and your planet will die tomorrow. How do you want to spend today?" Both Bringhurst and his co-author Jan Zwicky argue we must do the right thing even when we know our little lives will make no difference to the enormity of the problem. Moral decisions, moral gestures, moral behavior matter, Zwicky and Bringhurst argue, even when such decisions, gestures, and behavior might have no noticeable impact. We must try to do right for the sake of doing right — it's the only way to ward off apathy and despair.

We can hope that, collectively, all our little lives do make change.

"What would you say if I told you even our hiking and our camping do help the planet, in a way?"

Katie seems unusually quiet, maybe sleepy from her big day outside. In a rare display of affection, she rolls closer to my side and puts her head on my shoulder, her hair wet and cool against my sunbaked skin. "You mean," she says slowly, her words heavy with the effort of thought, tentative, "because . . . being outside more makes us . . . like . . . care about nature more?"

"*Yes*, don't you think so? I love nature. I believe you do too. All of *this*." I don't need to point at the lake and the mountains. We stay staring at the deep blue sky brushed by the tips of the forest. "People who *love* the world — both kids and adults — will do their best to protect it. You and I will do our best."

I pull her close, her damp suit cold against my rib cage, and I kiss her freckly forehead. "I love you so much," I say. Right now, that is all I can do.

I let it be enough.

Despite a looming book deadline, I have not brought pens and paper on this camping trip. I am not worried about pushing myself to that finish line, not on my last summer weekend with my family. These past few months, I have learned a new way to write, one that involves less urgency and less stress than my old ways. Instead of going to the page with a predetermined idea of what I want to say and how I want to say it, I go to the page and wait to discover what the page wants to say to me. The change in my process has grown out of the breathing lessons. I have been influenced by my breathing coach's advice that I should write to express what's in my heart, her encouragement to let myself be carried. Now, I think of writing as an intense form of listening. I remain open to possibilities. I let the process lead me.

I wonder if I could do the same with parenting. Maybe I could do the same with most of life. Instead of imposing my pre-conceived ideas of productivity and goals onto our family time, filling those hours with work deadlines and hockey schedules and swim-team commitments and peak-a-weak challenges, I could step back and see what life has to offer when I do not work so hard to give it shape and create an illusion of constant progress toward "success."

This weekend is nice. We do not check any boxes, achieve any goals, or tackle any challenges. Once I let go of my attachment to the kind of structure these goals provide, the illusions they create around meaning and progress and arrival, I enjoy the break.

"Marty. No. Honestly, you two. Give me strength! She is not water-skiing with a broken arm." While I will not win any best parent awards this weekend, I do finally decide to play enforcer, so at least I won't be the worst. The sight of my ten-year-old girl crouched in the ready position, half submerged in water, her hot pink cast flashing as she grips a rope attached to our friends' motorboat proves to be my breaking point. "Come on, Ms. Kat. Over here. You're done with adventure for today."

"Don't talk to me," Marty deflects when Kat turns his way. "Mom says. She's the boss."

I have to suck in my cheeks to stop myself from laughing as Kat storms my way. She lets the fire flare, living up to every red-head stereotype, and then some. "It's not fair!" She stomps her foot, slamming her fist into her thigh. "Everybody else gets to do it! *Everybody else!*" She throws herself into the sand. *Everybody else* means Ollie and our friends' one son. *Everybody.* All two of them.

Her theatrics are so far out of proportion, I finally do laugh. "Kat! You have a broken arm! Be realistic." This firecracker is the same girl we've labeled too timid? Too shy? "I'm glad you can speak up for what you want," I add. "But remember I am your mom. My job is to keep you safe."

She sits up and pulls her knees into her chest, water dripping down her body. She gives me one more hard scowl and then lets her forehead fall to her knees. The anger drains away until she's loose and sad. "I wanted to water-ski," she says to the ground, "like Ollie and Elliot."

"I know you did. Maybe we'll try water-skiing a different time." I sit down on the sand and put my arm around her wet shoulders. "This is not the weekend for water-skiing."

In this one short trip, I have seen all the versions of my girl. She has been silly and teasing her brother. She has been jubilant, leaping off the highest cliff. She has been strategically mature, presenting herself to our friends in a way that might lead to future babysitting work. She has been fierce, racing me in the lake. She has been intellectual, asking questions about climate crisis. She has been angry and sad when the day's events do not go as she likes.

"You know something?" I push my CamelBak into her hands and encourage her to drink some water. *Hydrate*; maybe in the end that's the most practical, helpful advice I can offer as a parent.

She tilts her head, cheek against knee, CamelBak tube in her mouth, wet hair falling into her eyes. "What?"

"I'm pretty proud of you. Even though you can't do everything today, I like your passion, the way you always try to do everything."

"Hmmph."

"Really. It's true. You have a zest for life. I like it. How about we compromise? I won't bug you about cliff jumping anymore this weekend. We're going to have to get your cast replaced anyway, so I'll give up on keeping you out of the water, if you give up on the idea of water-skiing."

She bites her lips and squints her eyes, thinking, and then she nods.

I call Marty, who's been watching us from his peripheral vision while Ollie water-skis. "Take her for a jump?"

"You bet!"

She springs up, happy again. Marty looks relieved at his Katie-bird's improved mood.

"Be careful, though," I yell after her. "Please." It's my favorite time of day, the light perfect, as if Kat moves through liquid gold. Still, she shines. I keep my eyes on her as she walks away, toward her dad. When she breaks into a jog, her arms and legs swing at comical angles. Nobody would ever call this girl graceful, but her awkward, intense movement fills me with joy. Her swim coach recently told me she is growing into her body like a little giraffe.

Her body is not all she's growing into. With immense grati-tude, I will watch this Kat person my daughter is becoming; I will get to know her in all her permutations. I'm aware now how little I control, but I will do my best to create a space where she can evolve into the person she wants to be.

"Hey," I shout after my little giraffe. "Katie! Hey! Kat!"

My daughter turns to look at me, holding her hand above her head to shield her eyes from the evening sun. I want a picture of her there, framed by the wide, beautiful world, the mountains and the lake and the sand and the forest.

A girl headed for adventure.

A soon-to-be-young-woman making the most out of her one wild life.

"I'll be right here," I smile at her, resisting the urge to tell her again how much I love her, "when you need me."

Selected Reading List

Bratman, Gregory N., J. Paul Hamilton, Kevin S. Hahn, Gretchen C. Daily, and James J. Gross. "Nature Experience Reduces Rumination and Subgenual Prefrontal Cortex Activation." Proceedings of the Natural Academy of the Sciences 112, no. 28 (June 2015): 8567-8572.

Breuning, Loretta G., "Nature Gave Us Four Kinds of Happiness," *Psychology Today*, July 6, 2007.

Bringhurst, Robert, and Jan Zwicky. *Learning to Die: Wisdom in the Age of Climate Crisis*. Regina: University of Regina Press, 2018.

Cain, Susan. "Is Social Media a Game-Changer for Introverted Kids?" *Psychology Today*, May 3, 2011.

Cain, Susan. Quiet: *The Power of Introverts in a World that Can't Stop Talking*. New York: Broadway Books, 2013.

Cori, Jasmin Lee. *The Emotionally Absent Mother.* New York: The Experiment, 2017.

Cullen, Nancy Jo. *The Western Alienation Merit Badge.* Toronto: Buckrider Books, 2019.

Farrey, Tom. "Does Norway Have the Answer to Excess in Youth Sports?" *New York Times*, April 28, 2019.

Firestone, Lisa. "Your Child's Self-Esteem Starts with You." *Psychology Today*, June 22, 2011.

Fisher, Nicole. "Your Brain on Drama." *Forbes*, August 10, 2018.

Frost, Joe. "Breaking Down Legal Barriers to Nature Play." Children & Nature Network, July 4, 2015.

Gadd, Will. "It's Never Too Early to Teach Kids Risk Management." *Outside*, April 22, 2019.

Gardner, Thomas. *Poverty Creek Journal.* North Adams: Tupelo Press, 2014.

Gaston, Bill. *Just Let Me Look at You.* Toronto: Hamish Hamilton, 2018.

Hartwell-Walker, Marie. "The Importance of Distraction-Free Parenting." Psych Central, October 7, 2018.

Heighton, Steven. *The Virtues of Disillusionment.* Edmonton: Athabasca University, 2020.

Jackson, Marni. *The Mother Zone.* Toronto: Vintage Canada, 2002.

Jensen, Kurt, Charlotte Nielsen, Claus Thorn Ekstrøm, Kirsten K. Roessler. "Physical Exercise in the Treatment of Alcohol Use Disorder (AUD) Patients Affects Their Drinking Habits: A Randomized Controlled Trial." *The Scandinavian Journal of Public Health* 47, no. 4 (June 2019): 462-468.

Knausgaard, Karl Ove. *My Struggle.* Toronto: Knopf Canada, 2016.

Lansens, Lori. *The Mountain Story.* Toronto: Vintage Canada, 2016.

Larkin, Philip. "This Be the Verse," in *High Windows*. New York: Farrar, Straus and Giroux, 2004.

Lee, J., Park, B.-J., Tsunetsugu, Y., Kagawa, T., Miyazaki, Y. (2009). "Restorative Effects of Viewing Real Forest Landscapes, Based on a Comparison with Urban Landscapes." *Scandinavian Journal of Forest Research* 24, no. 3: 227-234.

Manning, Richard. "Combustion Engines." *Harper's Magazine*, August 2018.

Martinelli, Katherine. "When to Push Your Children and How to Know If You're Pushing Too Hard." Child Mind Institute.

Marty, Sid. *The Black Grizzly of Whiskey Creek*. Toronto: McClelland & Stewart, 2008.

Murakami, Haruki. *What I Talk about When I Talk about Running*. Toronto: Vintage Canada, 2007.

Murdoch, Iris. *The Sovereignty of Good*. New York: Routledge, 2001.

Nhat Hanh, Thich. *No Mud, No Lotus: The Art of Transforming Suffering*. Westminster: Parallax Press, 2014.

Newport, Cal. *Deep Work: Rules for Focused Success in a Distracted World*. New York: Grand Central Publishing, 2016.

Nielsen, Linda. "How Dads Affect Their Daughters into Adulthood." Institute of Family Studies, June 3, 2014.

Oliver, Mary. "The Summer Day." *House of Light*. Boston: Beacon Press, 1990.

Peterson, Zoey Leigh. *Next Year for Sure*. Toronto: Doubleday Canada, 2017.

Price-Mitchell, Marilyn. "How Your Brain Finds Meaning in Life Experiences." *Psychology Today*, December 29, 2017.

Perel, Esther. *The State of Affairs*. New York: Harper, 2017.

Ronson, Jon. *So You've Been Publicly Shamed*. New York: Riverhead Books, 2015.

Sandseter, Ellen Beate Hansen. "Categorizing Risky Play – How Can We Identify Risk-Taking in Children's Play?" European Early Childhood Education Research Journal 15 no. 2 (June 2007): 237-252.

Sapolsky, Robert. *Behave: The Biology of Humans at Our Best and Worst.* New York: Penguin Books, 2018.

Sayare, Scott. "There Will Always Be Fires." *Harper's Magazine,* August 2018.

Shanker, Dr. Stuart. "When to Push a Child." *Psychology Today,* September 7, 2017.

Skenazy, Lenore. *Free Range Kids: How to Raise Safe, Self-Reliant Children (Without Going Nuts with Worry).* San Francisco: Jossey-Bass Publishing, 2010.

Smith, Steve. "Risk and Resiliency: How to Help Your Child Learn to Assess Risk." Children & Nature Network, June 10, 2015.

Spinoza, Benedict de. *Ethics.* New York: Penguin Classics, 2005.

Strayed, Cheryl. *Wild.* New York: Vintage, 2013.

Tronick, Ed. *The Neurobehavioral and Social-Emotional Development of Infants and Children.* New York: WW Norton & Company, 2007.

Tronick, Ed, and Claudia M. Gold. *The Power of Discord: Why the Ups and Downs of Relationships are the Secret to Building Intimacy, Resilience, and Trust.* New York: Little, Brown Spark, 2020.

Turk, Jon. *The Raven's Gift.* St. New York: Martin's Press, 2010.

Williams, Florence. *The 3-Day Effect.* Audible. 2018.

Williams, Florence. *The Nature Fix.* New York: WW Norton, 2018.

Wohlleben, Peter. *The Hidden Life of Trees.* Vancouver: Greystone Books, 2016.

Yamagata, Bun, Kou Murayama, Jessica M. Black, Roeland Hancock, Masaru Mimura, Tony T. Yang, Allan L. Reiss and

Fumiko Hoeft. "Female-Specific Intergenerational Transmission Patterns of the Human Corticolimbic Circuitry." *Journal of Neuroscience*. 36, no. 4 (January 2016): 1254-1260.

Acknowledgments

I wrote a big chunk of this book at Sharon Oddie Brown and Andreas Schroeder's beautiful ocean-side cottage, the perfect place. Thank you to two of the kindest and most generous people I have the good fortune to know.

The whole ECW team has made this project enjoyable, start to finish. Thank you especially to editor Susan Renouf, whose questions about *Home Ice* planted the seed for this project and whose comments on early drafts of *This One Wild Life* made it a better book. Thank you also to copy editor Rachel Ironstone for key catches, important insights, and good humor — this is the first time I've caught myself smiling through a line edit. Big gratitude to all the other enthusiastic professionals I'm lucky to work with at ECW (Jack David, David Caron, Jennifer Albert, Shannon Parr, Jennifer Smith, Emily Ferko, Caroline Suzuki, and Susannah Ames).

I'm also grateful to superstar agent Samantha Haywood for guidance, support, conversation, and friendship.

Andy Sinclair is too good to be true. Thank you, Andy, for reading every chapter I write as soon as I write it. Every author should be lucky enough to have an Andy (but they can't have mine). You're the best.

My writing group — the Fernie Five — came on this writing journey with me. They are *fantastic* company! Thank you Jesse Bell, Danielle Gibson, Coraley Letcher, and Keith Liggett (I'm the fifth for anyone concerned about my counting skills). That backwoods Montana #heycowboy writing retreat? Influential, unforgettable.

I'm also grateful for the friendship of Fernie writers Gordon Sombrowski and Kevin Allen, especially for their intellectual curiosity and deep insights. Ongoing conversations with them make my life more interesting and seep into everything I write.

Jowita Bydlowska, I'm sorry. Thank you. Wanna go hiking? We could do something big. <ducks> Which reminds me: Dave Hawrys — thanks from both of us, for the helicopter ride. I also owe big thanks to Fernie Search and Rescue, for obvious reasons.

Thank you to Richard Van Camp for an early reading and for always being so very positive, supportive, and lovely. I appreciate the collegiality.

Thank you to Monica Prelle for recommending Thomas Gardner's *Poverty Creek Journal* which served as inspiration, reminding me how much I like reading about deep-thinkers' relationships with nature and exercise.

Thank you to Fernie Heritage Library and Fernie Polar Peek Books and Treasures for keeping our little town's literary culture alive and thriving.

Fernie artist Laura Nelson and her cedar trees also snuck into this story. I'm grateful for her gorgeous paintings that help me appreciate the forest in new ways.

I have never in a book's acknowledgments thanked my two oldest friends — Robin and Robyn — because they exist so completely outside of my literary life. Events of recent years have taught me that's exactly why I should thank them. What would I do without you two? Chosen sisters. Unconditional love. Radical empathy. Easy forgiveness. Much laughter. Thank you.

I get obsessed with a book during my early drafts. Thanks to the tolerant friends and colleagues whose conversations shaped the project, especially: Gyllian Phillips, Hal Wake, Anna Hudson, Janice MacDonald, Sioux Browning, Douglas Brown, Tim Anderson, Kevin Patterson, Steven Heighton, Karl Subban, Ginger Pharand, Lorna Crozier, Kara Stanley, Glenn Dixon, Adriana Barton, Adele Weder, Jan Redford, Kate Harris, Karla Germaine, Deryn Collier, Janet McIntyre, Timothy Taylor, Richard Monette (and everyone else at Active for Life), Wendell Kisner, Desi Valentine, Sinead Murphy, Jon Turk, Matt Mosteller, and all my pals in the International Sport Literature Association.

Thank you to my colleagues and students at Athabasca University. I love my job because I love working with all of you.

Most of all, thank you to my family — the Abdous, especially my mom and dad, and the Hafkes. What fun we have. I am forever grateful that I get to share this one wild life with you. Marty, Ollie, Kat — you expand my heart. Here's to our next adventure!

Thank you, finally, to Mary Oliver for her poem "The Summer Day," which poses the famous question: "Tell me, what is it you plan to do / with your one wild and precious life?"